Marguerite duPont Lee
1910

THE SPIRITUAL UNREST

BY

RAY STANNARD BAKER

Author of
"Following the Color Line"
"New Ideals in Healing," etc.

NEW YORK
FREDERICK A. STOKES COMPANY
PUBLISHERS

Copyright, 1910, By
FREDERICK A. STOKES COMPANY

Copyright, 1909, By
THE PHILLIPS PUBLISHING CO.

All rights reserved

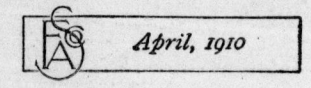

April, 1910

PREFACE

This book is written by a lay observer for everyday men and women, whether within the church or without. It is not an attack; neither is it a defense. It represents an effort to see the actual facts regarding actual churches and other religious institutions, and to set down those facts honestly and fully. The people can be trusted with the facts.

These chapters, here somewhat rewritten and rearranged, appeared originally in the *American Magazine*. The excuse for republishing them in a book lies in the large correspondence, both commendatory and critical, which they brought forth during their serial appearance, and in the many requests that they should be given a permanent form.

The author wishes to thank most heartily the many people both inside and outside the churches who have assisted him in his inquiries: he also expresses his appreciation of the many letters of helpful criticism and sympathetic suggestion which he has received.

The Religious Element

"The Religious Element is universal, immortal. . . . Every great revolution has borne its stamp and revealed it in its origin or in its aim. . . . The instinctive philosophy of the people is faith in God."

MAZZINI.

The Spread of Religion

"It is quite obvious that a wave of religious activity, analogous in some respects to the spread of early Christianity, Buddhism and Mohammedism, is passing over our American world."

PROFESSOR WILLIAM JAMES, of Harvard.

The Church

"The Church in reality is the society formed by those who claim fellowship with the Christ, and, above all, she is the still vaster society of those who, unconsciously and without knowing this blessed name, live in His spirit and continue His work."

PAUL SABATIER in "Modernism."

TABLE OF CONTENTS

PART I

CHAPTER   PAGE

I. A Study of Trinity — the Richest Church in America 1

II. The Condition of the Protestant Church 49

III. The Disintegration of the Jews — A Study of the Synagogues of New York City 101

PART II

IV. The Slum Mission and the Institutional Church: A Comparison of Their Functions 142

V. Healing the Sick in the Churches — An Account of the Emmanuel Movement 183

VI. The Faith of the Unchurched: Inspirations From Outside the Church . 232

VII. A Vision of the New Christianity — An Account of Professor Walter Rauschenbusch and his Work 260

THE SPIRITUAL UNREST

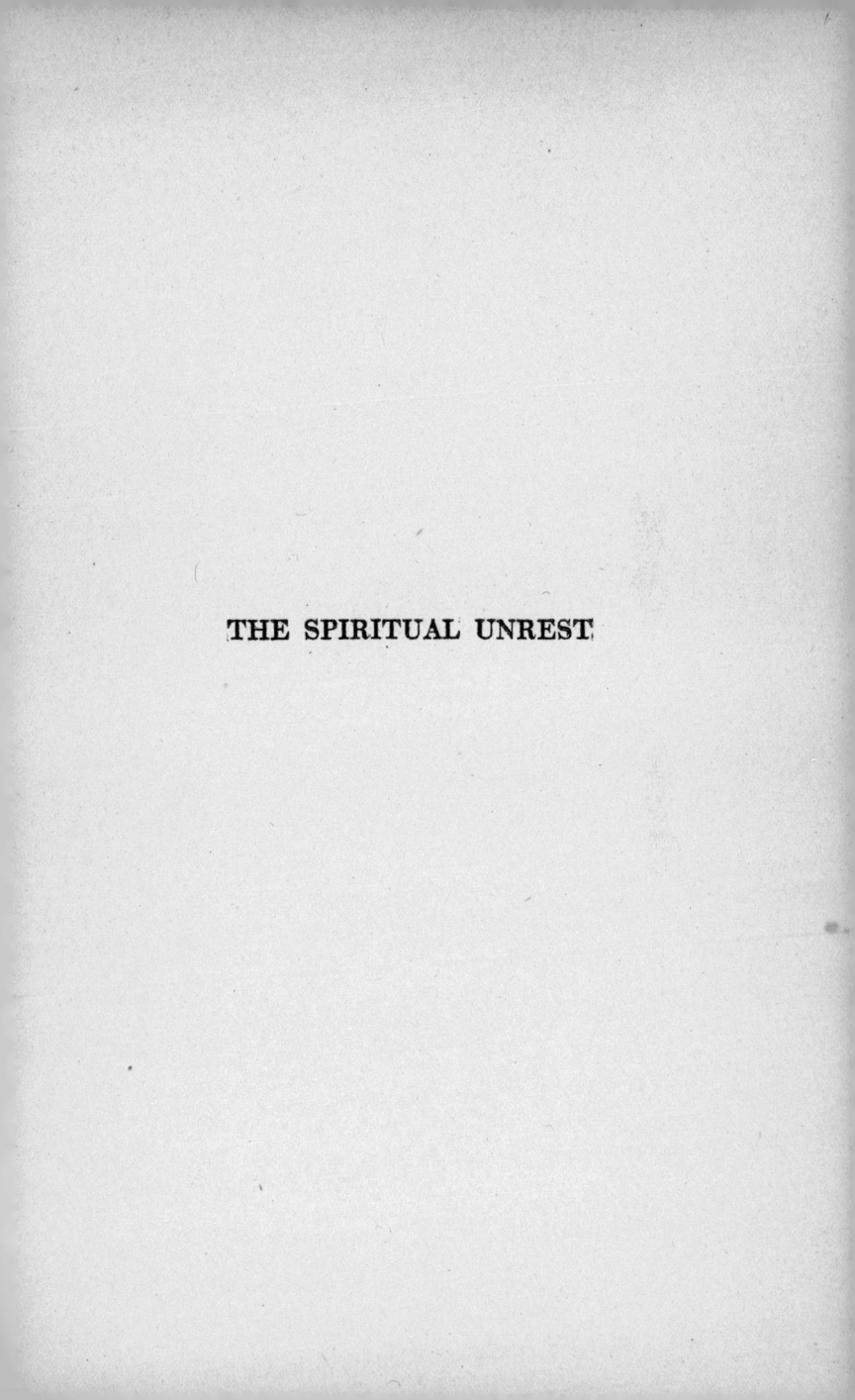

THE SPIRITUAL UNREST

PART I

CHAPTER I

A STUDY OF TRINITY—THE RICHEST CHURCH IN AMERICA

TRINITY CHURCH, which bears the enviable (or unenviable) distinction of being rich—the richest church in America—has been curiously under attack during recent months. Newspapers and magazines have presented its affairs in a light more or less unfavorable; its shortcomings have been discussed in not a few pulpits even in the Episcopal Church; the Legislature of the State of New York has been asked to consider its conduct as a corporate body; and finally, its distinguished rector and vestry have been summoned in the courts, and proceedings have been instituted which have been bitterly contested.

Is not this an extraordinary situation in which to find a great religious institution? Is it not strange that the public should be questioning the moral standards (for it comes to that) of the most notable church in America?

Let not, however, such questioning astonish us: it is neither unexpected nor unusual. That challenging of entrenched and wealthy institutions which has been proceeding so briskly for the past half dozen years has finally reached the last resort of conservatism: the church. Trinity, as everyone knows, lifts a presiding finger at the head of Wall Street. From its bronze doorway one can easily see the chief offices of the Standard Oil Company and the Steel Trust, and all about are the mightiest banks, insurance companies and other moneyed institutions of this half of the earth. Each in its turn—trusts, railroad companies, insurance companies—has been questioned, attacked, discussed in legislatures, haled into the courts. To each of these institutions democracy has put its blunt queries (is putting them to-day):

A STUDY OF TRINITY

Are you serving the people, or, are you serving your own selfish interests? What are you doing that you should be retained as the approved tool of civilization?

Nor should it surprise us to find that democracy stands knocking at last at the closed doors of Old Trinity, nor to hear it asking:

What, then, have *you* done with the talents we gave you? Have *you* been a faithful servant?

I shall here set down the facts regarding Trinity Church; nothing that I could write, indeed, would illuminate more clearly the prevailing condition of spiritual unrest in this country, nor present more graphically the dilemma of the church in our modern life.

What, then, is this Trinity Church?

WHAT IS TRINITY CHURCH?

Every human institution has one supreme function: to serve the people in one way or another. A railroad corporation serves by carrying freight and passengers; a church serves by promoting the true spirit of religion. In order to perform its service to the people properly, a railroad corporation is provided with certain tools—depots, a road-bed and rolling stock, and a church has its spired building, its music, its preaching, its schools. A church is not religion: it is a mere human agency for fostering religion. It may contain the Ark of the Covenant, or it may not. When the people, then, arise to criticise the church, they are not attacking religion, but rather the public service of the institution which assumes to promote religion. It is as proper to ask of a church as of a railroad company: Is it doing its work efficiently?

Like many of the great trusts and corporations, Trinity has become inordinately wealthy. No church in the world, perhaps, has so much property and such a varied and costly equipment. The value of its property is beyond $50,000,000. Of this about two-thirds is distinctly church property, untaxed: for Trinity parish not only owns the magnificent church which stands in the midst of the spacious and beautiful (and enormously valuable) old churchyard at the head of Wall Street, but it owns and conducts nine other churches some of them nearly as large as Old Trinity itself. It also owns a number of church houses,

A STUDY OF TRINITY

school buildings, a hospital, and a cemetery, all of which are included in its list of untaxed church property. This vast machinery of service is controlled by Trinity parish, a corporation similar to other business corporations, except that the directors are known as vestrymen, the general manager as Rector, and the stockholders as communicants. Like many other corporations, Trinity has a large income-producing investment outside of its actual operating plant. About one-third of its property—to the value of over $16,000,000 (assessed value, as given in the Trinity report, $13,646,300)—is in rented lands and tenements. In short, it is a big business corporation: calling it a church does not change its character.

One of the deepest, if not the deepest, need of men is religion; hence from the beginning of time men have encouraged and built up institutions to respond to that need with service. No other human institution has been so sedulously fostered or so lavishly maintained as the church. One of the very first things that our forefathers did upon coming to America was to set up churches: and one of the earliest

THE SPIRITUAL UNREST

churches so set up in New York Colony was Trinity. It was established in 1697—two hundred and thirteen years ago. It was fostered then, and it has been encouraged since, exactly like any other public service corporation—only with a greater degree of generosity. In the early days of railroading, for example, the people were so eager to extend the service of transportation throughout the country that they gave to railroad corporations vast grants or "bonuses" of land, they presented them with free franchises conveying special rights and privileges, and they even exempted railroad property from taxation.

TRINITY OBTAINS A FRANCHISE.

In exactly the same way Trinity Church was built up. In 1697 a franchise was granted to Trinity to build a church "situate in or near the street called Broadway," and it was to be "for the use and behoof of the inhabitants from time to time inhabiting or to inhabit within our city of New York, in communion of our protestant church of England." Eight years later came the "bonus" or grant of land, then called the Queen's farm, which extended picturesquely along the Hudson River on the west side of Manhattan Island. This tract, now densely covered with human habitations, was then practically uninhabited. Since then for over two hundred years that part of the property used for church or educational purposes has not been taxed. It has been calculated that the remitted taxes on Trinity Church property for the last two hundred years—the free gift of the people of New York regardless of creed—would amount to many times the present total value of the property of Trinity.

For many years Trinity acted literally according to the provisions of its franchise. It gave money and land freely to other struggling churches; assisting them first as chapels and as soon as they were strong enough to stand alone, Trinity gave them its blessing and made them independent. St. George's, Grace Church, and other important churches began thus with help from Trinity.

But the city of New York began to grow: the Queen's farm, at first of little use to Trinity, became more valuable. Other churches were organized, and, as usual where large property values are at stake, a difference of opinion began to arise as to who should control it.

The original grant had been made, as I have shown, to all "of the inhabitants of our said city of New York" in communion with the Church of England. Naturally other churches than Trinity thought they should have a share of the property: but Trinity would not release its grip. And in 1814, the vestrymen of Trinity succeeded in getting a law passed by the New York Legislature which at one stroke limited the control of the property to "members of the congregation of Trinity Church, or of any of the chapels belonging to Trinity corporation." This was the first step in a long process of centralizing and narrowing the control of the property.

After 1814 the policy of the great church began to change. Instead of serving all the inhabitants it devoted less and less of its income to the building up of outside churches and spent more and more on its own services. Instead of helping a chapel to become independent and self-governing, it established

A STUDY OF TRINITY

chapels and kept absolute control of them. In 1814 it had only two dependent chapels—St. Paul's and St. John's; to-day it has nine.

All this time the property of Trinity was growing more valuable. The Queen's farm had been cut up into blocks and lots; whole streets had built up with fine residences and places of business. The rental income of Trinity corporation increased enormously. Of course Trinity Church did absolutely nothing to earn this income, except to hold the title of the land: the people of New York who moved into and developed that part of the city were the real producers of the income.

BEGINNING OF THE MOVEMENT UPTOWN.

As the money began to pile up, Trinity bethought itself how to spend it. Many of its well-to-do members were moving uptown, so the corporation appropriated what was then (1852) the enormous sum of $230,000 to build Trinity chapel in West Twenty-fifth Street, together with a beautiful residence for the clergy. That act brought forth a storm of protest. It was shown that Trinity had deserted mission work in the lower part of the city where the mass of the people lived, where its own property was located, and diverted the money to the building of a church for the uptown rich. These rich people, of course, might have built a chapel of their own; the poor people downtown whose rentals helped to make Trinity rich could not afford to build churches. The glaring injustice of such an act brought about an inquiry by the legislature, and William Jay, a son of the great chief justice, and one of the most prominent citizens of New York (he was the grandfather of the William Jay who is at present senior warden of Trinity Church), wrote a stinging letter to the Rector of Trinity, in which he said:

"Wealth is naturally defiant, and so long as you can lengthen your rent roll and multiply your thousands, and purchase submission and obsequiousness, you may afford to look down with supercilious indifference on the complaints and disaffection of those who are impotent to injure you. But sir, there are signs in the political horizon which threaten a coming tempest which may level the proud pinnacles of Trinity in the dust."

A STUDY OF TRINITY

Mr. Jay also charged that Trinity was using its wealth not "for the permanent benefit of the church" but for building up the influence of the "high church" party in the Episcopal Church, there being at that time a heated conflict going on between the two factions in the church. Said Mr. Jay:

"Her wealth has in this city, in the opinion of many, been lavished in ostentatious buildings, rather than used in promoting true piety and religion; and the parochial reports have given ground for most unfavorable comparison between the number of communicants and the amount of benevolent offerings in Trinity and her chapels, and various other churches in the city."

Trinity continued to grow richer. In 1890 the corporation went still further uptown, following the rich, and built the magnificent church of St. Agnes in West Ninety-second Street, at a cost of about $500,000. In the meantime it had built one large chapel downtown—St. Augustine's, in Houston Street—and afterward it acquired another, St. Luke's, on the lower West Side.

THE SPIRITUAL UNREST

HOW TRINITY HAS CONTROLLED ITS GREAT PROPERTY.

How has Trinity controlled all of this great property? It is controlled, like that of the life insurance companies, by a board of directors, here called the vestry. The vestry is elected by the stockholders—here called communicants, but not all the communicants by any means are voters. Originally, under the law of 1814, every member of Trinity or its chapels had a vote; but the process of narrowing control has here also been going on. Under a law passed in 1867 (supported in the legislature by Trinity) churches are granted certain powers to establish free chapels. Under this law five dependent chapels were organized having no voice in the affairs of Trinity Church. Not one of the chapels in the poorer districts now has a vestryman; in fact, Trinity corporation is controlled by the two rich chapels: St. Agnes and Trinity Chapel, all the vestrymen being selected from these two chapels and from Old Trinity.

One of the most remarkable conditions brought out in the Hughes investigation of the life insurance companies was the fact that their boards of directors were practically self-perpetuating bodies. Nominally they were elected by the policy holders and stockholders: but as a matter of fact few policy holders were ever present, and the elections were controlled absolutely by the men in power.

Such is the case with Trinity corporation. Though there are many hundreds of communicants entitled to vote at the Trinity elections, comparatively few ever attend. At one election the twenty-two members of the vestry were elected with a total of twenty-three votes. The vestry has been in effect a self-perpetuating body, controlling an enormously valuable property, making no public reports at any time, and oblivious to criticism either from within the church or without.

What was the result of the control of such a self-perpetuating, irresponsible board of vestrymen who could be reached by no criticism?

It was very little different from the result in other corporations. Perhaps it was, if anything, worse, because there was less accountability on the part of the board of directors (vestry). An Insurance Department at Al-

THE SPIRITUAL UNREST

bany made at least a pretense of supervising the insurance companies; but there was no Church Department at Albany—no one on earth who had any power to demand any sort of an accounting from Trinity corporation. And unlimited power over vast unearned property in the hands of a few men who are not accountable to anyone can work out in only one way—whether the men are organized under a churchly name or not.

And what is that result?

THE DISEASE OF UNEARNED PROPERTY.

A curious, insidious, benumbing disease seems to afflict those who control unearned property. Subtle psychological changes take place within them. One might expect such men to say to themselves: The people have endowed us with special franchise privileges; they have granted us land to work with; they have built up this land and increased its value; they are paying us a large yearly income; they have remitted our taxes for over two hundred years. We therefore owe them the most enthusiastic service, and the frankest

A STUDY OF TRINITY

accounting of our stewardship. Do they say this? Not at all. By the curious psychological change to which I have referred, they come to act as though the property which they control was in reality their own. They resent any questions regarding it; they spend the income where and how they like; they make no accounting to anyone.

But these men of the vestry of Trinity are high-class men. All of them are educated men, some belong to very old families, some are famous, nearly all are wealthy. Many are connected with various good works (see their names in the Charities Directory). All of the twenty-two (except the controller and the clerk) contribute their services, they receive no salary. Not one of them can be suspected of profiting by so much as a penny from the business transactions of Trinity parish. I suppose, indeed, the same thing can be said of the directors of life insurance companies, railroads and banks—who are also high-class men. Indeed, many of these rich vestrymen of Trinity are actually in the directories of great business corporations (see their names in the "Directory of Directors"); they are part and parcel of the current methods of doing business.

In the life insurance investigations what were some of the discoveries made? It was disclosed that the business was extravagantly conducted; that inordinately high salaries were paid; that gorgeous and expensive offices were maintained; that the men in control made conditions highly comfortable for themselves and their friends. A curious parallelism exists between the life insurance companies and Trinity.

People ordinarily expect to pay something, make some self-sacrifices for their religious advantages. Some of the most heroic stories in the world are told of the sacrifices of men and women to build up places of worship, but the congregations of Trinity parish get their religious advantages practically for nothing. According to the financial statement issued recently by Trinity (the first public report in over fifty years) it cost $340,870 to maintain the ten churches and the schools of Trinity for one year. Of this vast sum the members of all the churches contributed just $18,210

A STUDY OF TRINITY

(in pew rents). All the remainder of the expense was met from the rental income from the property owned by Trinity. In other words, the poor people and other tenants on Trinity lands have paid not only for the support of the chapels in the poorer part of town, but they have built the rich uptown churches and are paying practically all the running expenses. Communicants in Trinity worship in churches which they have not built, and to the support of which they contribute practically nothing. They are, in short, religious paupers.

It is true that the congregations of Trinity churches contributed during the year $94,000 for special charities—but none of this money went to church support, and even if it had been so applied it would not have begun to liquidate the cost of operating the churches.

Music alone cost Trinity last year (including care of organs) $63,000, or over three times as much as all the members contributed to the entire support of the church. There have been many complaints of the Trinity tenements (of which more later), but at least they pay for a great deal of fine music—

also for twenty-eight clergymen at a cost of $101,674 and for thirty-two sextons and engineers at $26,555. I find an item of "fuel and light for churches" of $12,280. The total contributions of Trinity communicants for church purposes ($18,000) will pay *that,* and some to spare.

As in the life insurance companies, salaries range high, the Rector is said to receive the highest salary of any clergyman in America, $15,000 a year, and some of the vicars receive $8,000 each—more than the salary of a United States senator. Besides the salaries many of the clergy also receive free residences (on partially untaxed property), so that they have no rent to pay—a big item in New York City— and when they retire they are generously pensioned!

It was found in the life insurance companies that, although keen business men conducted the operations, some of the real estate owned yielded a very low income. The same is true of Trinity. It costs just short of $50,000 for salaries and office expenses in conducting the real estate business of Trinity, and yet the net income last year on $16,000,000 worth of real

A STUDY OF TRINITY

estate was only about $376,000 (gross $752,000)—or a little more than two per cent. Tenement house property in New York is ordinarily expected to pay from five to six per cent. net, and other rented property not less than four per cent. Judging even from a strict business point of view, then, Trinity corporation is certainly open to severe criticism. The management of a private estate which could show earnings of only two per cent. would speedily be turned out, but Trinity, not making public reports, no one could know how the vestry was conducting its trust.

WHAT OF THE TENEMENTS.

I come now to the tenements. A great deal has been written and said of these tenements during the last twenty-five years. Many years ago the Trinity houses were occupied by rich or well-to-do people, but to-day they are crowded with wage-earners of all sorts and of many nationalities. While other parts of the city were built up to new buildings, these old houses on Trinity property have largely remained, although, in recent years, Trinity has put up a number of new business buildings and warehouses. There is no more barren, forbidding, unprogressive part of the city than the Trinity blocks south of Christopher Street. Trinity has sat still and waited for the increase of the value of its land.

Well, old buildings are old, and the city has been progressing in nothing more than in tenement house reform—in short, in its views of the responsibilities of the city to the poor and unfortunate. A distinctly higher standard of social morality has been built up in New York in the last twenty-five years. And in its work of improving conditions in the crowded districts of Manhattan Island the city authorities have repeatedly collided with Trinity corporation. The first clash came in 1887. A law had been passed requiring that running water should be furnished on each floor of tenement houses. In most of the Trinity houses the tenants had to go down stairs and out of doors to get their water supply. When the demand was made on Trinity to obey the law, the vestry objected and began a bitter fight in the courts, which finally reached the Court of Appeals. Of course this costly litigation was not paid for by the vestrymen or even by the

A STUDY OF TRINITY

communicants of Trinity. This legal battle was financed out of the rentals of the very people who were to be benefited by the new law.

However, it was an epoch-making case, the decision of which will long be quoted, for it decided that the state can compel a private owner, for the good of the public to alter a house at his own expense. But the church had to be driven to the new moral standard by the courts. Here is the way in which Judge Peckham, afterwards appointed to the Supreme Court of the United States, laid down the law to Trinity:

"We may own our property absolutely and yet it is subject to the proper exercise of the police power. We have surrendered to that extent our right to its unrestricted use. It must be so used as not improperly to cause harm to our neighbor."

But Trinity's long-fought legal battle had succeeded in delaying the enforcement of the law from 1887 until 1895—eight years. In spite of itself, however, Trinity helped along the cause of better homes for the poor in a way it little intended. The very bitterness of its legal struggle against making improvements served to turn public attention even more closely to housing conditions in lower Manhattan. In 1894 the famous tenement house commission, of which Richard Watson Gilder was chairman, was appointed. Investigation showed that hundreds of tenements had no toilet conveniences in them, but that so-called "school-sinks," or open water closets in the back yards, were used by all the tenants, and that thousands of men, women and children were sleeping in dark holes of rooms in which there were no windows opening to the outer air—breeding places, indeed, for tuberculosis.

In 1901 a law was passed through the efforts of the Tenement House Commission of which Robert W. De Forest was president abolishing "school-sinks" and dark inside rooms in tenements. Trinity waited; this time the law was tested in the courts by another landlord, and it was not sustained until 1904. What did Trinity then do? Where it could not avoid compliance with the law, necessary changes were made, but in many cases it slid out of making improvements through a provision which defines a tenement house as any

A STUDY OF TRINITY

building occupied by more than two families. In some of the old houses where there had been more than two families, Trinity reduced the number to two, and thus by getting out from under the tenement law, was able to refrain from making the repairs demanded.

TRINITY FIGHTS IMPROVEMENTS.

Trinity has always been against improvement; it has always had to be lashed to its moral duty by public opinion or by the courts, or by fear of legislative action. Even when the city was seeking for land for the children's play-ground at Clarkson and Houston Streets on the West Side, it had to enter into a long and costly fight in order to get the land from Trinity corporation.

As to the condition of the Trinity tenements I made a careful investigation of many of them. They are not so bad as I expected to find, no worse than those owned by other landlords in the same neighborhood. In general, they are better—and why shouldn't they be? Why should such ancient tenements have been allowed to remain at all? In general, the rents are low, and in many cases they have not

THE SPIRITUAL UNREST

been raised in twenty-five years. And this much must be said to the credit of Trinity; none of its property is rented for saloons or for immoral purposes. There are only two places on Trinity land where liquor is sold, and in those cases the property is under a lease which cannot be controlled by Trinity.

Over and over again, when complaints have been made of Trinity houses, the vestry has said:

"We are not responsible; the land is leased and the building is owned by the lessee. We cannot control it."

And yet when the leases expire, it has been, in the recent past, a custom of Trinity to relcase for two years to the owner of the building. Of course no such owner can afford to make repairs when he may lose his building in two years and he does as little as possible. Trinity thus gets its land rent, the landlord gets his house rent—and the tenant who pays the bills gets just as bad a place to live in as the Board of Health will permit.

It is difficult, indeed, to see how a group of men individually so intelligent and honorable should collectively exhibit so little vision, so

A STUDY OF TRINITY

little social sense, so little justice. Whether judged as good morals or as good business, the results have been lamentable and disheartening.

Complaint has been widely made (especially in New York City) that the church was losing its hold on the people, that people do not go to church as they once did nor take the interest in religious affairs that they should. Has the position of Trinity with its low standards of social justice and morality had anything to do with that tendency? When the public and the courts, and the legislature, have to castigate a church to higher moral standards, why should the people go to church for instruction? What inspiration has the church to give? Spending $63,000 a year for music and $340,000—mostly taken from the poor—to support its churches, it has been willing for many years, until brought to a realization of its duty by the force of law, to let at least some of its poor sleep in disease-breeding dark rooms and suffer for the want of sanitary conveniences. How, under such circumstances, can it preach a lowly Saviour and the love of man to man?

WHAT TRINITY DOES WITH ITS MONEY.

Perhaps I have now dwelt sufficiently upon the business side of Trinity. I come now to the service which it performs. However extravagant or corrupt the administration of life insurance companies had become, the Hughes investigation showed that they yet performed a service; they paid losses.

So Trinity performs a wide and varied service. Every Sunday in all the ten churches the usual religious services are held, and there are also the usual Sunday Schools and weekday meetings. I have attended, at various times, most of the Trinity churches. Some of them are well attended, some not so well; and the audiences are just about what one finds in the ordinary New York church.

Besides the regular worship there are also the usual missionary and philanthropic societies, sewing classes, kindergartens and many clubs for young people. One of the interesting and valuable activities of St. Paul's Chapel is a working girl's club which furnishes a meeting and luncheon place in one of the church buildings. But perhaps the most extensive single department of the activity of Trinity outside of its strict religious work is the day schools. There are seven regular day schools connected with seven of the churches—somewhat similar to the parochial schools of the Roman Catholics. A manual training, cooking and drawing school is maintained in Washington Square and there are three night schools. All this work is free to pupils, the only obligation being that the children shall attend Sunday School. The work follows closely that of the public schools, save that a certain amount of religious instruction is also given. School work cost the parish last year $63,755.

What does Trinity do for churches and charities outside of its own parish? As I said before, the congregations of Trinity contributed $94,000 last year for various charities and benevolences. But Trinity corporation itself, which was chartered to minister to all the inhabitants of New York in communion with the Episcopal Church, contributed only $46,579 to churches and charities outside of the parish—or less by some $17,000 than it paid for music in its own churches. It also made

THE SPIRITUAL UNREST

one loan of $5,000 to help a church outside of the parish. One of the regular expenses of every Episcopal church is the apportionment made for the general mission work of the church. Old Trinity was supposed to pay $10,000. It never met this amount: three years ago the general church reduced the apportionment to $2,500, so that Trinity would pay, but never until last year did it meet even this amount. It has, indeed, been notorious among the churches of New York for shirking its missionary obligations.

TRINITY LOSING IN MEMBERSHIP.

Judged by its own statistics, Trinity has lost ground. It has been unable to maintain its membership, in spite of the vast sums of money expended, the costly music, the activities of an army of workers. Old Trinity in 1898 had 1,767 communicants; in 1908 it had 1,340—a loss of 427 members in ten years. The figures for the combined church and chapels (except one, acquired since 1898) are scarcely less encouraging. In 1898 the total was 7,220; in 1908 it was 6,939—a loss of 281 members in ten years.

A STUDY OF TRINITY

Now, I am acutely conscious, having made this dry, catalogue-like report of the work of Trinity, with its statistics and its cost, that I have not told the whole story of service. I appreciate fully the difficulty of measuring spiritual values. The work of an insurance company or a railroad can be measured more or less accurately by statistics. Not so, a church—even though the clergy themselves are content to appeal to statistics of membership to prove their efficiency. Often I have stepped into the dim coolness of Old Trinity from the roar of Broadway on a busy day and found men and women kneeling in silent prayer. Who shall measure the value to individual human souls of such a place of refuge and worship? Or who, indeed, can compute the incalculable influence of the quiet old churchyard itself—the beauty of it, the calm of it—with its suggestion of eternal values in a place where men are furiously pursuing immediate gain? Nor can any one of us pass judgment upon the service of the individual workers in Trinity—the clergy, the vestrymen, the sisters.

And yet it is not at all a question as to

whether Trinity is doing spiritual service. Of course it is. But should it not do far more? Have its leaders that breadth of vision without which the people perish? Has it power of leadership in our common life? Is it making the best use of its tremendous opportunities, its enormous wealth?

These are fair questions; questions which, indeed, the most earnest men within the Church itself are asking. They are questions which the public at large has a right to ask.

With the idea, then, of presenting the specific facts, I have studied, somewhat carefully, the methods in two or three of the Trinity churches. And I wish here to show how the work is done.

In the first place, the people in the churches have nothing whatever to say as to the conduct of their own affairs. Everything is provided for them by the self-perpetuating autocracy which controls the property; their music is paid for; their ministers are hired by Trinity. The people have nothing at any point to say. Last November a whole congregation—that of St. John's Chapel—was informed one Sunday that the church would shortly be closed,

A STUDY OF TRINITY

and all the people were told that they could go to another church. No one had been consulted, there had been no chance of protest or explanation; the chapel, which had been open for one hundred and two years, was ordered closed. But of St. John's more later.

Even in the rich chapel of St. Agnes, when Dr. Manning was promoted to be Rector of Trinity, the new vicar was chosen by the vestry before the congregation had ever heard him preach. Thus every detail of the machine is managed, not by the people, but by the benevolent autocracy at the top.

USING MONEY TO PROMOTE RELIGION.

Consider, for a moment, the work of one of the chapels in the poorer part of town. I give these facts hesitatingly, because the clergy are earnest men working in the deadening toils of a system which destroys inspiration and quenches brotherly enthusiasm—and yet the truth must be set down. A large proportion of the people connected with that chapel get something out of it in cash or in material benefits. And I say this advisedly, knowing that many individuals love this chapel and receive spiritual advantages from its work. Every member of the choir, of course, is paid a regular stipend. To encourage the Sunday School officers one hundred dollars in cash is distributed among them every year. Last Christmas, that day of spontaneous giving, the corporation appropriated $750 for decorations, a tree, and gifts for the people. The Sunday School is made up largely of the children who are being educated (free) in the day and night schools conducted by the chapel, and are therefore *compelled* to attend Sunday School. And it may be said, further, that the day school pupils are also encouraged by prizes—so they, too, get something out of it.

Besides these regular payments, the dispensation of charity of various sorts undoubtedly assures the connection of not a few people with the church. It is one of the emphasized rules of this chapel that "assistance is given only to persons that are regularly enrolled members of the chapel cure."

This particular chapel has a staff of twenty-six clergy, teachers, lay-workers and sextons regularly hired, and a choir of twenty-four members—a total of fifty paid workers. Yet

A STUDY OF TRINITY

I have been in that chapel during services when there were not fifty people in the congregation. Think of it! With land and buildings worth $300,000 and an operating cost (I could not get the exact figures) of probably not less than $50,000, although it is in a neighborhood swarming with people, this is the use to which it is put! A little money—very little—is collected from the congregation for charities, but not one cent is paid by the people of the church for the support of the work. It is pure charity.

Do not think that the people in the neighborhood who see this sort of work do not know exactly what is going on. No people are more sensitive to real values, or quicker to see the difference between charity and brotherly love, than these people of the tenements. Charity is indeed often necessary, but it requires the genius of love to bestow it properly. One woman, a member of a Trinity Chapel—one of the clean, self-respecting, hard-working sort, an example and a light in her neighborhood—gave me this point of view in so many words:

"There is too much giving. Most of the people go there to get something; they don't expect to help. The tendency is to pauperize the people and cheapen the real meaning of religion."

No, the people are not fooled.

When I asked a clergyman in Trinity why so much was given to these people and so little required of them, I was told:

"Why, they are poor; they can't help."

"THEY DESPISE THE PENNIES OF THE POOR."

He said that the church had discontinued certain of its collections because the people gave only pennies! He thought they should be discouraged in making such small offerings! "They despise the pennies of the poor."

From this very chapel I went down to Baxter Street—not far away—and visited a Catholic Church—the Church of the Most Precious Blood. It is a large new church, with a lively, able priest at the head of it. It is attended exclusively by Italians—the poorest people in the neighborhood, and yet that church has been built complete in fifteen years out of the pennies of poor people, and it is supported to-day by their offerings. I am not here entering into a discussion of the Roman Catholic sys-

A STUDY OF TRINITY

tem; I am merely pointing out that poor people can and do contribute to religious work, when that work really means something to them.

Nor need I make a comparison only with the Roman Catholics. I have a still better example: a Protestant church on the lower West Side, not far from two of Trinity's chapels, St. John's and St. Luke's, and ministering to the same sort of people. I refer to the Spring Street Presbyterian Church, the work of which is like the shadow of a rock in a weary land. The Spring Street Church ministers wholly to wage-earners, the average wage of the membership being less than ten dollars a week—and the highest wage of any member being eighteen dollars a week. While both the Trinity chapels still have a few well-to-do people in their congregations, the Spring Street Church has none at all. And yet, while Trinity paid last year $20,000 to operate St. John's Chapel, Spring Street Church was wholly self-supporting. When the Rev. H. Roswell Bates, its minister, went to the church eight years ago, he told the feeble congregation that he would enter the work only upon condition that every expense (including his own salary) was met by the people of the community. The members got together and resolved to work as they never had before. Some of them went without eggs and butter all the first year, others walked to their work to save car fare, in order to help raise the amount necessary. And the church has grown rapidly both in membership and in influence. Last year the congregation contributed $4,900 and maintained an active and enthusiastic work for six hundred and thirty-five members. The church has become a marvelous source of power in the community; everybody works for somebody else; everybody gives, rather than gets. They have now built up a neighborhood Settlement House next the church, where there are many clubs, classes, a kindergarten, a day nursery and the like, largely conducted by volunteer workers. Money from the outside is contributed to help maintain the settlement work, but the church is supported wholly by the congregation.

While the Spring Street Church supports its work for 635 members with $4,900, Trinity pays $20,000 for 487 communicants at St.

A STUDY OF TRINITY

John's chapel. And this is not making an unfavorable comparison of St. John's as against other Trinity chapels: for the work at St. John's, cost for cost, is probably more profitable than at most of the other chapels. At St. John's the music cost $6,000—more than the entire cost of the work at the Spring Street Church. St. John's has six paid clergymen and lay workers, while the Spring Street Church has three.

STORY OF ST. JOHN'S CHAPEL.

In what I have said about St. John's, let me not blame the clergy. They were earnest young men; they had to labor against the paralysis of the Trinity system, and in spite of that they had been broadening their work. They had increased the number of communicants of the chapel, and they had built up guilds and classes of various sorts. I wish to make this point particularly, because I come now to the story of St. John's Chapel. As every one knows, Trinity attempted to close St. John's Chapel in the fall of 1908 and precipitated a storm of agitation.

St. John's Chapel is one of the oldest

churches in New York; a beautiful building, once in a fashionable quarter of the city, now surrounded by warehouses and tenements. One Sunday in November, 1908, the curate in charge read a notice from the pulpit to the effect that the vestry had ordered the church closed on February first, and that the congregation would be expected to attend St. Luke's Chapel—a mile further north. It came like a thunderbolt out of a clear sky. Trinity corporation, probably looking about to reduce expenses, had thus, by executive order, cut off a chapel with four hundred and eighty-seven communicants, and a Sunday School of three hundred and twenty-one members, in a neighborhood where many of its tenements were located, and from which it drew nearly all of its income. Its excuse was that the work, considering the changing character of the neighborhood, and the influx of foreigners, no longer paid, that the money could be better expended elsewhere (perhaps on the rich churches uptown), that the congregation of St. John's could easily go to St. Luke's and the work of both chapels could go forward together.

A STUDY OF TRINITY

A storm of protest at once arose. A petition from the members of St. John's was presented to the vestry respectfully asking that their committee be granted a hearing and the St. John's Chapel be not closed. It was ignored. The members then presented a second petition, in which they said:

"The request accompanying our former petition, that a committee appointed by the members of St. John's chapel be granted a hearing, has been ignored. We have no representative on the vestry. Years ago, five of the vestrymen were members of St. John's Chapel, but owing to the movement of wealthy people to uptown districts, the vestry seems now to be largely selected from members of the Chapel of St. Agnes, located on West Ninety-second Street, leaving us with no representation. Bishop Potter, a friend of St. John's Chapel, and the late Rector, the Rev. Dr. Dix, who dearly loved it, are no longer with us; and our beloved Vicar, who has ministered to us for more than thirty years, is absent on account of ill-health. The present rector has been in the city of New York but a few years, during which period he has resided in the upper part

THE SPIRITUAL UNREST

of the city; and we believe he has not had occasion to become familiar with conditions existing in the neighborhood of St. John's Chapel. Since he has been rector we have not seen him at any of the services of St. John's Chapel, and the first and only communication we have received from him was the notice which was read from the pulpit that the doors of the church would be closed February first, 1909."

AN APPEAL TO THE BISHOP.

The committee also appealed to the Bishop of the Diocese, Bishop Greer, and finally offered on behalf of the congregation to take over and support the church themselves. Still Trinity corporation did not budge.

Then the public began to stir. A notable memorial was presented to the vestry on behalf of St. John's; it was signed by the most distinguished citizens of New York, among them President Roosevelt, Secretary Root, Mayor McClellan, Ex-Mayor Seth Low, Joseph H. Choate and others.

Other memorials were presented by the New York Art Commission and the Fine Arts' League. The Municipal Art Commission asked "respectfully and earnestly" that the corporation might further consider "whether in the public interest St. John's Chapel, as a landmark of the early religious and social life of the city, and as a work of art, might not be permanently preserved and maintained as a place of worship."

One of the most impressive and powerful appeals was a poem written for the New York *Evening Post* by the late Richard Watson Gilder. It was called "Lines on the Proposed Demolition of St. John's Chapel." It is published here:

LINES ON THE PROPOSED DEMOLITION OF ST. JOHN'S CHAPEL

By Richard Watson Gilder

Guardians of a holy trust
Who, in your rotting tenements,
Housed the people, till the offense
Rose to the Heaven of the Just—
Guardians of an ancient trust
Who, lately, from these little ones
Dashed the cup of water; now
Bind new laurels to your brow,
Fling to earth these sacred stones,
Give the altar to the dust!

THE SPIRITUAL UNREST

> Here the poor and friendless come—
> Desolate the templed home
> Of the friendless and the poor,
> That your laurels may be sure!
> Here beside the frowning walls
> Where no more the wood-bird calls,
> Where once the little children played,
> Whose paradise ye have betrayed,
> Here let the temple low be laid,
> Here bring the altar to the dust—
> Guardians of a holy trust!

And finally, Trinity spoke. Three defensive statements were made, one by Trinity corporation itself, one by Bishop Greer, and one by Dr. Huntington, rector of Grace Church. It is significant that neither the Bishop nor Dr. Huntington had ever investigated the condition of the people of St. John's nor the work being done there, yet they defended the action of Trinity as being "in the interests of the Christian religion," to quote from Dr. Huntington. The *Churchman* says of these three statements:

"But the distinguishing characteristic of the three statements is that nothing is said of the people in St. John's parish, of their rights, of their hopes or of their souls. Even the ap-

A STUDY OF TRINITY

peals that have been made in their behalf have been ignored. What religion means under such conditions, the public are left to guess."

Not having investigated, neither these men nor the Rector of Trinity, could know the real love with which many of the members of St. John's clung to their chapel. Here is the brief story of one of the communicants:

"I have been a regular member and contributor of St. John's Chapel, in good standing, for more than twenty-five years. The religious life largely of my immediate family has been connected with St. John's Chapel. My only brother was confirmed there and he died twenty-two years ago and his funeral services were held there. My sister was a communicant at St. John's Chapel; she was confirmed there, and was married in that church. My mother was confirmed there; she died about fourteen years ago, and her funeral services, also, were held in that church. In that church I met my wife, who was baptized and confirmed there, and our marriage ceremony was performed in that church, and our two children have been baptized there, and one of them, my boy, is at present a choir-boy in St.

John's Chapel. My wife and I have both taught Sunday School in St. John's Chapel, and my wife is now and has been for some time a delegate to St. Augustine's League from that chapel."

The plain fact is that Trinity did not care for the people. And it was not really until the agitation had grown to such an extent that legislative and judicial action were threatened that Trinity began to move. Then it was too late to prevent the whole matter from being carried into the courts. The people of St. John's based their case on the declaration that under the charter of 1814 they were voters in Trinity parish and that the closing of St. John's and the relegation of the membership to the free-mission chapel of St. Luke's deprived them of their franchise rights, and they demanded redress from the courts. A temporary injunction was immediately issued ordering Trinity to keep St. John's Chapel open for religious services. The litigation, however, is likely to be long continued and very bitter. On the side of the people the cost of the cases will have to be raised by general subscription where money

A STUDY OF TRINITY

is not plentiful; but it will cost the vestrymen personally not one cent; they will use the ready money of the church—which comes out of the rentals from the very neighborhood served by St. John's Chapel. Their chief lawyer is himself a vestryman, paid by the vestry.

RESULTS OF THE AGITATION AGAINST TRINITY.

Several excellent results, however, have come out of the agitation. First, Trinity corporation has shown the first evidence in its history that it feels any responsibility to the public. It has issued a public report defending its position in closing St. John's Chapel, and giving its first financial statement in over fifty years. It has also declared its purpose of doing away with the old tenements as rapidly as possible and improving the land with new buildings. It has also decided to open St. John's Chapel on week-days, and provide noon revival services for the people of the neighborhood.

I have talked with many of the people connected with Trinity in various capacities. I found them all disturbed—indeed, astonished, perplexed, and unable to account for the extent and violence of the public agitation. One of them said it was "jealousy of the wealth of Trinity"; another blamed the clergy of St. John's; another laid it up to "agitators." They did not seem to understand, to have any grasp of the new spiritual impulses which are permeating our common life—the new democracy, if you will—and they are yielding just as they have in the past, grudgingly, without vision. They are paralyzed by their own wealth and the pride of their traditions. They would like to improve things— a little—but they do not see that the whole aristocratic, feudalistic system upon which they are operating belongs to a past age, that religion is not charity, but justice and brotherly love. They are not ready to make the self-sacrifice necessary, in the highest sense, to save the life of their church.

It is, indeed, not at all surprising to hear the clergymen of rich and doctrine-bound churches strike the note of disheartenment. They themselves often work hard, with a passionate earnestness of devotion, but they do not get spiritual results. The church is not holding its own; people avoid the church.

A STUDY OF TRINITY

The clergy wonder why; they ask vainly, "What is the matter with the church?" It even seems to some of them that religion itself is decaying.

But religion is not decaying; it is only the church. More religion is to be found in our life to-day than ever before, more hearts respond to its inspiration; it is found among common men and women everywhere. As ever, it demands, not observances, nor doctrines, nor a habitation in magnificent temples—but self-sacrifice and a contrite heart.

Thus earnest men in Trinity find their efforts paralyzed by wealth and tradition. They are very far away from life, these poor men of Trinity; they have not felt the thrill and inspiration of the new time. By and by they will find it impossible to listen to beautiful and costly music, which they have not paid for, without thinking of the people of the tenements, and of the men and women and the little children there who must work long hours at low wages, and out of whose small earnings comes the money to pay for that music. And they will see the absurdity of taking from the people of the tenements and giving nothing back—save empty homilies. "It will become a matter of wonder that there should ever have existed those who thought it admirable to enjoy without working, at the expense of others, who worked without enjoying."

CHAPTER II

THE CONDITION OF THE PROTESTANT CHURCHES

FOLLOWING the presentation in the last chapter of the "Case Against Trinity Church," the question naturally arises:

"What about other churches in New York City and elsewhere? Are they or any of them triumphantly successful in reaching the masses of the people? Do any of them sound the clear note of spiritual leadership? Is their service adequate to the conditions of the new age?"

In order to answer these questions with clearness I have spent many months visiting the churches and missions of New York City and indeed of other cities and towns; I have talked with many clergymen and other leaders in religious work; I have visited settlements, charity organizations and labor unions in

THE SPIRITUAL UNREST

order to get a point of view of the churches from the outside; and finally, I have made a somewhat careful study of the abundant literature issued by the various denominations

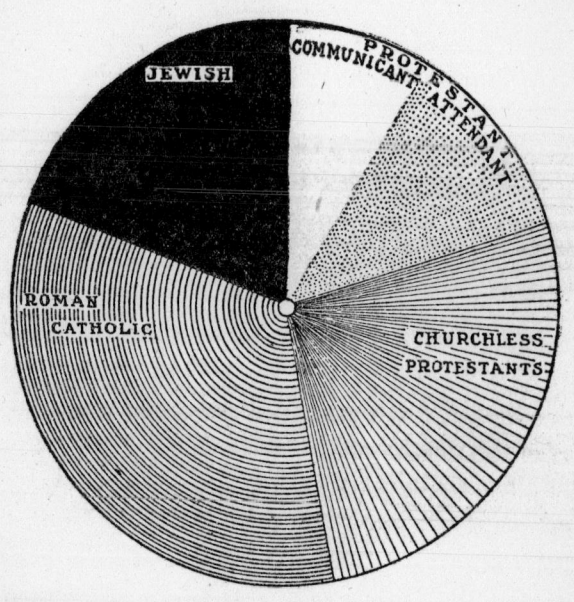

Diagram showing proportion of Roman Catholics, Jews and Protestants, in New York City.—*From The Federation of Churches.*

regarding church conditions in New York City. In this article I shall give an account of the general conditions and tendencies of church work as I have found them.

THE PROTESTANT CHURCHES

One of the most extraordinary things that I discovered when I began the study of the church situation in New York City was the very general tone of discontent and discour-

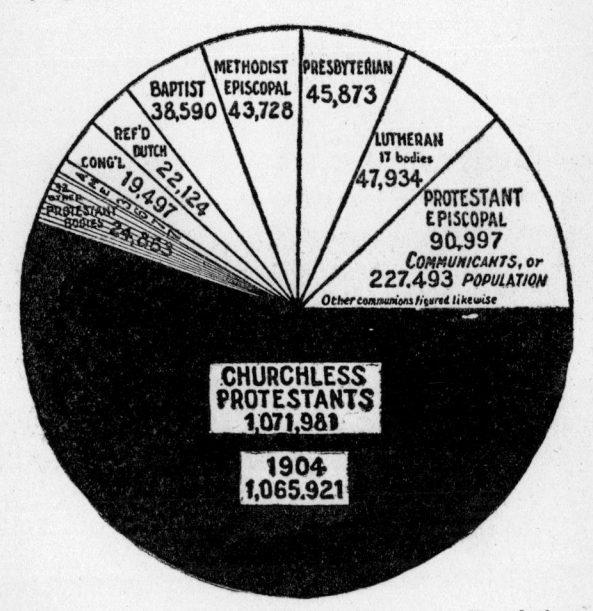

Diagram showing the Division of Protestant Population of New York City in the year 1905.— *From the Federation of Churches.*

agement among church workers themselves. They feel that the churches are somehow inadequate to their great task of spiritual leadership. Something is felt to be wanting.

THE SPIRITUAL UNREST

The Reverend Charles E. Jefferson of the Broadway Tabernacle, the oldest and one of the largest Congregational churches in the city, said last year in a sermon:

"While the church has been filled with doubts and fears, there has been an ever deepening estrangement between the church and large classes of our population. . . . The last decade has been the most strenuous and discouraging for Christian workers which this city has probably ever known."

Not long before his resignation, broken down with overwork, Dr. Rainsford of St. George's Episcopal Church struck the same note of despondency—calling attention to the falling away in the size of the Sunday congregations in spite of the most strenuous activities to keep the work at white heat. The late Reverend George C. Lorimer of the Madison Avenue Baptist Church said in one of his last sermons:

"There is such a thing as a religious crisis in America, however much we may scoff at the idea. Religion is to-day of very low vitality."

THE PROTESTANT CHURCHES

ONE MILLION CHURCHLESS PROTESTANTS.

Many other New York ministers have made statements of similar tenor which are, indeed, substantiated more or less definitely by the findings of the Reverend Dr. Walter Laidlaw of the Federation of Churches, who has made extensive sociological and statistical studies of church conditions in New York City. Dr. Laidlaw estimated that in 1905 there were over a million (1,071,981) churchless Protestants in the city. By churchless Protestants are meant people whose antecedents were Protestant and who, if they became interested in religious work, would naturally associate themselves with some Protestant church. Dr. Laidlaw shows, moreover, that the membership in Protestant churches, in spite of rapidly increasing population, has barely held its own in Greater New York, while on Manhattan Island there has been an actual loss of membership.

In the first five years of this decade (1901–1906) the population of Manhattan Island increased by 300,000, but the number of Protestant church buildings actually decreased by three, the Catholic churches increased by only five, and the Jewish synagogues (buildings), in spite of the enormous Jewish immigration, by eighteen.

The Roman Catholic Church has felt a similar loss of power, not only in New York, but in other great American cities. Concerning this tendency we have the word of no less a personage than Archbishop Falconio, apostolic delegate from the Pope, spoken at the first great missionary conference of the Roman Catholic Church in America, held last spring in Chicago. He said:

"In our day a spirit of religious indifferentism and relaxation of Christian morality is permeating the sanctuary of Christian families. To check this dangerous tendency we need a revival of the true Christian spirit. Besides, in some dioceses numerous Catholics are in want of priests, churches and schools; there are immigrants who are in need of religious assistance."

And the Roman Catholic is not more concerned than the Jew. Although the Jewish population of New York City is growing rapidly, the same disheartenment exists among Jewish religious leaders as among Christians. The Jews, especially of the younger generation, show a growing inclination to drift away from the synagogues and the teaching of the fathers.

A clear observer, the Reverend Charles Stelzle, superintendent of the labor department of the Presbyterian Church, who sees the church from the point of view of the workman, says:

"The church to-day seems to have arrived at one of the most crucial periods of her history. . . . No one can successfully deny that the church is slowly but surely losing ground in the city. Nearly every city in America is witnessing the removal of its churches from the densely populated sections where the church is most needed. Within recent years forty Protestant churches moved out of the district below Twentieth Street in New York City, while 300,000 people moved in. Alarmed for her safety and her very life, the church has sounded a dismal retreat in the face of the greatest opportunity which has ever come to her."

THE SPIRITUAL UNREST

Not only have the working classes become alienated from the churches, especially from the Protestant churches, but a very large proportion of well-to-do men and women who belong to the so-called cultured class, have lost touch with church work. Some retain a membership, but the church plays no vital or important part in their lives. Thousands of men and women who contribute to the support of the churches, yet allow no church duty to interfere with the work or pleasures of their daily lives. They are neither inspired nor commanded. And what is more, this indifferentism is by no means confined to the "wicked city" but prevails throughout the country, in small towns and villages as well as in large cities—except possibly in a few localities where "revivals" have recently stirred the people.

DECLINE OF THE COUNTRY CHURCHES.

That the same tendency toward decline of power exists in the country as in the city is thoroughly well established, not by opponents or outside critics of the church but by some of the ablest and most loyal of church leaders

THE PROTESTANT CHURCHES

themselves. We have for example, a circular letter sent out by the Reverend F. N. McMillan, Chairman of the Committee on Evangelistic work of the Presbyterian Synod of Ohio, in which it is said:

"The net increase of communicants in our Synod has been declining for many years, so that last year it was only eleven hundred and fifty-two. This is nearly fifteen hundred less than it was five years ago. This shows that we are not doing much more than holding our own.

"One presbytery of three thousand, nine hundred and forty-one members received on examination, only one hundred and thirty-eight. Ninety-eight churches received none and many less than five.

"The records demonstrate that the Church as a whole has declined in efficiency for the past eighty years. In the first third of the last century we seldom added less than ten per centum on examination and the rate sometimes went up to fifteen and even eighteen. Even under pressure of the Assembly's Committee, the highest reach has been only a little over seven per centum, but this was equaled or exceeded in thirteen different years since 1870. All of these facts indicate a general condition that calls for the most serious consideration.

"It is an ungrateful task to present a view of the apparent condition of the church within this synod. The attendance on Divine Worship is nowhere what is desired, especially on the part of children and youth. The evening services are very generally neglected, both on the Sabbath and at the midweek meeting. Family worship is almost unknown. The general tone reveals a lack of deep interest."

CHURCHES IN RURAL DISTRICTS.

As to the distinctly rural church the Rev, Dr. A. S. Fisk speaks in the New York *Observer,* a religious journal, of the dwindling away of many old country churches by difficulty in maintaining their list of membership and by financial embarrassment. Many of the farmers, he says, whose ancestors regularly attended church, no longer keep up any religious form of observance. "To cope with these conditions," the writer says, "requires something more than traditional methods."

THE PROTESTANT CHURCHES

PROBLEMS OF THE THEOLOGICAL SEMINARY.

Another significant sign of weakening power lies in the fact that able young men are no longer attracted to the ministry as they once were. The theological seminaries have had a hard time to hold their own. Recently the Reverend Dr. J. M. Barkley of Detroit, Moderator of the General Assembly of the Presbyterian Church, called attention to this condition in an address before the Michigan synod. He said that beginning in 1825, there was an average of one young man to every 800 communicants entering the Presbyterian ministry. That average held good until 1895, when the ratio fell to one for every 1,400. Of late years there has been a slight improvement, and the ratio is now one to 1,176.

RECENT GOVERNMENT CENSUS OF CHURCHES.

Recently the government has issued a census report of religious conditions in America. It shows, generally speaking, that church membership between 1890 and 1906 had a little more than kept pace with the population, the Roman Catholics gaining more rapidly—by

THE SPIRITUAL UNREST

immigration, of course—than the Protestants. And yet, some extracts from a careful review of this census report written by a minister, the Reverend Dr. Henry Davies, and published in a religious journal, *The Churchman,* will show how this census is regarded even by religious critics.

"Some people, perhaps, will derive several small crumbs of comfort from the facts revealed in this report; but taken as a whole it is impossible not to be discouraged and alarmed. . . .

"It helps us little in the ultimate difficulty to learn that there are (counting baptized members) 33,000,000 persons enrolled in the churches of the United States. Still less are we encouraged by the fact that a billion and a quarter dollars are invested in church edifices; that does not help us to a believable faith and to sound ethical views, even about money; it is simply a sign of the wealth of these corporations, most of them untaxed and many of them dodging taxes. Still less is the critical situation helped by learning that considerably less than half the total church membership is formed of men.

THE PROTESTANT CHURCHES

"The ultimate difficulty as revealed by this report, is unaffected by these figures, from which, as I said, few can derive comfort. The question is: Is the church to continue going down hill? or will she yield to the critical process, which is encompassing her, by making the needed adjustments to adapt her to become once again our fundamental social force?"

I have not here quoted from enemies of the church, from infidels, or free-thinkers, but in every case from leaders of the church, who have the best interests of the church at heart.

Another difficulty the church has had to meet is that of financial support.

I was surprised, not long ago, when I asked one of the foremost church laymen in New York City what, in his opinion, was the trouble with the churches, why the churches were losing ground, to hear this reason advanced:

"Money. We can't get money."

By this, he said, he did not, of course, mean to imply that money in itself would make a church successful or the lack of it would necessarily mean failure.

THE SPIRITUAL UNREST

"But money giving," he explained, "that is, spontaneous money giving, is the surest evidence of vital human interest. A man does not voluntarily give his good dollars to a cause unless that cause really stirs him, and we in the churches must face the fact that people are no longer giving to the churches as they once did."

This remark set me to examining somewhat carefully the long lists of bequests and benevolences of the past few years in this country, and I have been astonished to find how completely the great streams of voluntary and spontaneous giving have been diverted from the churches, and from church work generally.

During the past ten or twelve years the almost inconceivably enormous sum of one billion dollars has been given away by Americans for various philanthropic purposes. Of this stupendous sum comparatively little went to the churches.

HOW MILLIONAIRES GIVE THEIR MONEY.

Rockefeller, for example, although an exuberant church-member, has given comparatively little money to church work. He has

THE PROTESTANT CHURCHES

been interested in outside activities, chiefly educational and medical. Mrs. Russell Sage has been distributing her millions not among the churches which have been gradually deserting the poor, but she establishes a great fund for studying methods of improving the conditions of the poor, or she purchases an island in the Hudson River and dedicates it to the United States government. Carnegie builds libraries which are open not only to Protestants, but to Catholics, Jews, Mohammedans, Negroes. No lines are drawn. Phipps builds model tenements and D. O. Mills model hotels for improving the living conditions of people of small means. Last year Morris K. Jesup died. He was one of the most loyal of Presbyterians, but of his gifts not one-tenth went to church work, while nine-tenths was given to outside activities like the American Museum of Natural History. And Mr. Jesup's proportion for churches was very large compared with that of most givers. Even many Roman Catholics who have left fortunes have contributed not exclusively to the church as they probably would have done twenty or fifty years ago, but have favored all sorts of public causes. A wealthy Roman Catholic woman recently left considerable sums of money to Jewish institutions!

The largest single gifts to a church—and they were magnificent—were more recently made by John Stewart Kennedy, who also gave largely to outside educational institutions.

Not only the dollars of the rich but the pennies of the poor have been diverted in large measure from the church. No one can study even cursorily the Socialist movement, the trade-union movement, the spread of fraternal and mutual benefit societies, without being impressed with the great sums (in the aggregate) which are being given yearly to maintain these movements. Almost the only distinctive church activity in which I have found any considerable growth or spontaneity of giving is the Christian Science movement.

BUSINESS METHODS OF THE CHURCHES.

And at the same time that money is being so readily and so generously bestowed upon all manner of outside activities, the churches are having to devise complicated and organized methods of getting money from people,

THE PROTESTANT CHURCHES

Churches are to-day advertised like business enterprises; several books have been written on church advertising and promotion which reveal the most adroit business methods of attracting people. In New York I saw really impressive systems of card-catalogues and other business devices among the churches for keeping in touch with contributors. A formidable number of publications and speakers are constantly at work stirring up enthusiasm, urging people to contribute money. More and more either the Bishop, the clergyman, or some member of the board of trustees must be an energetic business man. More and more large churches are seeking the safe haven of endowments; they fear the future.

Notwithstanding all these activities, however, there is a cry of underpaid clergy and ill-supported work. More and more it has been found necessary to take a larger proportion of the money given to the church to pay maintenance expenses—thus cutting down the proportion appropriated for benevolences.

Examine for a series of years the reports of almost any church or denomination in this country which gives adequate financial statistics and it will be found that, although the country has been increasing enormously in wealth, the contributions to many churches have either actually fallen away or else have crept forward at snail's pace. It will also be found that some churches are using more in proportion of the money collected on themselves, less on benevolences. Here are statistics of gifts for a twelve year period of four great denominations (from "Social Progress," edited by the Rev. Dr. Josiah Strong).

	Benevolences Per capita		Home Expenses Per capita	
	1893	1905	1893	1905
Baptist, regular	$1.15	$0.65	$2.06	$3.01
Congregational	4.88	3.24	13.16	13.54
Methodist Episcopal	.85	1.04	5.62	6.21
Presbyterian	5.14	4.71	12.52	12.35

Of course many prosperous outside activities have been inspired from the churches, and many of the leaders to-day are either members of the church or were in younger days brought up and inspired by the churches. And for this the churches should have the fullest credit; but the evidences of former power and leadership does not prove that the church is now growing in power and leadership. We are try-

THE PROTESTANT CHURCHES

ing to find out the state of the church *now*, and the tendencies which are manifest *now*.

One group of activities like the Christian Endeavor Society, the Epworth League, the Brotherhood movement and the Y. M. C. A. are still actively religious and adhere more or less closely to the churches; but it is significant that the organizations which are now growing fastest and seem most prosperous, like the Y. M. C. A., have departed furthest from church influence and place the chief emphasis not on distinctly religious work, but on social and educational activities and physical training. Even the Salvation Army, beginning as an emotional religious revival, has become a great agency for providing employment, lodgings and food for poor people. Its Christmas dinners and its lodging houses are perhaps more noteworthy now than its religious activities.

Perhaps the greatest and most successful branches of church work are the missionary associations and missionary activity, especially the very remarkable laymen's movements. In some ways the church situation is more hopeful in China than it is in the United States. Many of the brightest of the graduates from the theological seminaries prefer to go to the foreign field because the opportunities seem brighter and the work freer.

Now I do not wish to imply for an instant that there are not strong movements under way to make the church more useful, more a power in one common life. I shall, indeed, present some of the ways in which the church is now endeavoring to re-establish itself as a commanding influence, but the point I make here is that the church leaders themselves testify to the declining condition of the churches. The very fact, indeed, that they do see it, and that they are willing to present the truth boldly and fearlessly is in itself the most encouraging feature of the whole situation. It requires rare qualities of courage for a man within an institution which he venerates, which is to him a real part of his life, to admit the weakness of that institution, especially to those who are outside. Whether a church, a political party, or a business corporation, the "insider," the leader, must of necessity be a defender. And it is hardly too much to say, now, that these critics within the church, these

THE PROTESTANT CHURCHES

Isaiahs and Hoseas of the church, who cannot be blind to the truth regarding conditions, are the best hope of the church. For self-criticism is the beginning of progress.

Such, in general, are the conditions at the present time, to which the church leaders themselves are the strongest witnesses. We may now look into the causes of this decline of church influence, narrowing our study in the present chapter to the Protestant churches of New York City.

FLIGHT OF THE CHURCHES AWAY FROM THE PEOPLE.

One of the most evident tendencies of Protestantism in New York City has been the movement of the churches uptown, or out of town, following the movement of the rich or well-to-do people. In fact, the Protestant churches for over a century have been in a constant condition of flight away from the common people. Where poor people, or foreigners, or Jews moved in, the Protestant churches moved out. Apparently they were afraid of foreigners, afraid of the poor, afraid of Jews, afraid of Catholics.

THE SPIRITUAL UNREST

But the churches, though in constant flight, always looked back. They did not leave the masses of the people without qualms of conscience. They felt that, as Christians, they had a duty to perform toward the poor and the foreigner, though they did not want the poor or the foreigner in their comfortable churches. They wanted to help him—on their own terms and at a respectable distance.

To fulfill what they felt to be a duty toward the poor, the Protestant churches long ago devised a business-like plan for "saving" them. A number of the denominations came together in 1825 and organized the New York City Mission and Tract Society, and a few years later the Episcopal denomination on its own account organized the City Mission Society.

Not for a moment would I minimize the work done through many years and still being done by these organizations, but the fact remains that they were institutions paid by the churches to perform the service of human brotherhood—"to visit the fatherless and widows"—which the churches themselves would not or did not do.

In the sixties the population in the lower

THE PROTESTANT CHURCHES

part of the city had grown so dense that it was felt that more efficient means must be taken to reach, religiously, the masses of the people. Accordingly the Mission and Tract Society began building mission chapels—the first, Olivet Memorial Church, in 1867. They planned to take over more of the work of salvation, assuming, indeed, the general territory below Fourteenth Street on the East Side. Since then they have largely extended their work.

Two things happened after this. First, a still more rapid hegira of the churches from the lower part of the city to the comfortable residence districts uptown. In the forty years after 1867 no fewer than seventy-two churches and missions moved uptown or perished. The following are the denominations:

Baptist	11	Episcopal	12
Congregational	1	Dutch Reformed	5
Methodist	16	Universalist	2
Presbyterian	14	Others	11

In short, there has been a gradual separation, a drawing apart, of the churches of the rich, and the chapels and missions of the poor.

After 1867, indeed, this tendency was greatly accelerated by the development of dependent missions by the rich Protestant churches which had moved to the comfortable uptown residence districts. Either the consciences of the leaders were troublesome, or else they looked with apprehension to the establishment of non-denominational churches by the Mission and Tract Society; at any rate the movement toward building missions for the poor was widespread. The rich churches usually paid for everything outright. They furnished the church, they hired the minister, they paid for the music—and then they marveled because the poor did not flock into the missions and be converted. It is a fact that many of these missions have had a precarious and discouraging career. The Reverend Gaylord S. White, of Union Theological Seminary, who has seen much of the work of church missions, says of them:

FAILURE OF MISSION CHAPELS.

"The misconceived mission chapel, unattractive and often positively mean in appearance, but 'good enough for the poor' and fitted out with a pastor to match—the whole

THE PROTESTANT CHURCHES

thing undemocratic and insulting in its implications to the intelligence and self-dependence of the workingman—has been a dismal failure."

But the uptown churches, having paid their money for mission work among the poor, were apparently content.

Be it far from me to decry the unselfish work often done by earnest men and women in these missions, nor shall I fail later to show how the work of some of them has recently been improved. I am merely making the point that they did not, after all, reach or influence any considerable number of people. Children came, and women and a few men, but the population at large was apathetic, if not openly hostile. An old mission worker told me that it was a common gibe among the people of the neighborhood in his earlier days to ask of a person seen going to the chapel: "Have you got your basket with you?"

Many excuses are made by the Protestant churches for their present discouraging and decadent condition in New York City. No one will deny that the situation has been enormously difficult to meet. Thousands of

Roman Catholics and Jews have been pouring into the city every year and settling districts formerly occupied by Protestants; a self-absorbed, amusement-loving city life is difficult to reach religiously, and to a large extent the population is in a state of flux, moving about so rapidly that it is difficult indeed for a church to keep in touch with its people.

Yet, while all these difficulties are recognized, the fact remains that the Protestant churches have been losing ground in New York—have failed to meet the great problem of the twentieth century city. Even if the Protestant leaders would admit that their faith is not broad and deep enough to apply to any but a certain class of well-to-do people of Anglo-Saxon or Teutonic stock, which of course no Protestant *will* admit, the fact remains that the Protestant churches have not been able to maintain even the allegiance of their own people. As Dr. Laidlaw shows in the statistics I have already referred to, there were in 1905 over 1,000,000 nominal Protestants in New York City who had no church affiliations. On the other hand, they have been practically unable to reach any of the

THE PROTESTANT CHURCHES

enormous Jewish population, although a large proportion of the Jews—eighty per cent. in some parts of the city—are themselves alienated from their synagogues. Through foreign-speaking missionaries, the Protestants have reached a few Roman Catholics; but, on the other hand, the Roman Catholics have probably reached quite as many Protestants.

It is advanced as an explanation of the conditions that the Protestants have migrated in large numbers to the suburbs where they have built up thrifty churches—but this is not so much an excuse as a further illustration of the flight of the Protestant churches away from the poorer people. Attempts have been made to interest the suburban churches in the conditions in the crowded districts of New York, but so far practically with no success. Although the members of these suburban churches come into New York every day, employ more or less directly many of the people of the crowded districts, and make their money in the city, yet they apparently feel no responsibility for religious conditions there.

Naturally, this flight of the Protestant churches, or their lack of adaptability to modern conditions, has not gone unnoted. In a very true sense the Protestant churches and Protestant doctrines are on trial—as many religious leaders recognize.

HOW THE CHURCHES MET THEIR PROBLEM.

Years ago, the uptown independent churches which of course dominate their respective denominations in the city, began to feel that ordinary mission work was not enough. What *was* the trouble? This was a question familiarly asked in public and religious conferences; it was discussed with heat in religious journals—and variously answered.

The first instinct of the rich, whether individuals or a church, when really troubled, is to *give more money*. Money to the rich somehow seems the universal explanation.

And this was the method first attempted in New York City. When an institution is young it possesses abounding vitality, it has hope and faith, it is more or less oblivious to material expression or to material comfort. But when the institution grows old and fearful, begins to lose its confident hold upon life, instinctively it seeks to replace its failing vigor

THE PROTESTANT CHURCHES

with material proofs of its greatness and power. As the spirit dies down, stone buildings rise up. As I have gone among Protestant churches in New York, as I have studied their abundant literature, I have discovered both clergymen and layworkers in many cases devoting a very large part of their time, not to progressive religious work, but to getting together huge sums of money which, put out at interest, will support the work of their churches. No longer able to command the enthusiastic allegiance and the willing offerings of the people, they resort to the ready alternative of interest-bearing stocks and bonds.

The struggle for money, indeed, is often fierce enough! Here, for example, is the plea in a Methodist publication on behalf of the "twentieth century movement" among the churches of New York:

"This movement is primarily an effort to secure money. The goal fixed, a million for Metropolitan Methodism, makes the enterprise a worthy one, worthy of the marvelous century into which we have come, of the city in which we live, of the denomination to which we belong, its traditions, its history, its spirit; worthy of the coöperation of all our people, challenging our largest loyalty, our most venturesome courage, and our unshrinking faith. . . . All the methods employed have been simple and straightforward. The strong motive of self-interest was appealed to, for self-interest is always stronger than public interest."

Yes, the methods have been simple and straightforward, and self-interest has been appealed to.

A CATHEDRAL OF THE RICH, FOR THE RICH.

Another expression of the same tendency is to be found in the upbuilding of enormous and costly churches, cathedrals and parish houses. The new cathedral of St. John the Divine (Episcopal) is a notable example of what I mean. Set upon the top of a hill five miles up the Hudson River from lower Manhattan Island, it is isolated in every possible way from the crowded centers of population. An enormous, pretentious structure, it will probably cost when completed over $20,000-000. It has been constructed in imitation of

THE PROTESTANT CHURCHES

the great cathedrals of Europe, but instead of being a people's church, paid for by the people and growing out of a passionate religious and democratic impulse, as did those wonderful old cathedrals, this huge and costly temple, built by the subscriptions and bequests of rich men and rich churches, is indeed far removed from the spirit of the age. Says Paul Sabatier of the middle age cathedrals:

"The cathedrals were the lay churches of the thirteenth century. Built by the people for the people, they were originally the true common house of our old cities. Museums, granaries, chambers of commerce, halls of justice, depositories of archives, and even labor exchanges, they were all these at once."

How far is the Cathedral of St. John from realizing any such democratic idea!

Nor is this movement toward great buildings confined to the Episcopal Church: the Presbyterians have been trying to raise money to endow one of their churches in Fifth Avenue as a sort of Presbyterian cathedral, and some of the newer churches of other denominations are of exceeding gorgeousness and costliness.

THE SPIRITUAL UNREST

More money is being put into endowments and permanent funds than ever before; but in spite of this inflow, the churches have steadily lost influence.

Although the population of the city has been increasing, although the number of missions has risen, although the amount of money expended by this denomination has increased, the report of the Methodist Church Extension Society of New York City for 1908 will show that the mission church and Sunday-School membership of this progressive denomination has been slowly declining.

	Number of Churches, Missions and other agencies	Number of Members	Number of Conversions	Number of Sunday School Scholars
1890	24	3,439	1,181	7,101
1895	25	3,465	1,082	6,496
1900	23	2,815	531	4,054
1905	28	3,048	536	4,187
1907	28	3,216	640	3,901

While some of the Methodist missions of 1890 are now self-supporting churches, the fact remains that the mission work of 1907 was not as productive for the church, as a church, as that of 1890.

THE PROTESTANT CHURCHES

The same tendency is shown in nearly all other denominations. For example, in the Episcopal Church, Sunday-School enrollment, which is a good barometer of church interest, has been falling away in spite of the utmost activity to maintain it. Here are the recent figures for New York diocese:

Sunday School enrollment in 1900...................... 44,226
"   "   "   1904...................... 43,974
"   "   "   1908...................... 38,840

Of this falling off in Sunday-School enrollment a member of the Sunday School Commission said:

"Great parishes on Manhattan Island are losing their schools, or some of them are. Children of well-to-do parents rarely attend, and even the less well-to-do are growing increasingly careless. New York is the largest and among the first to suffer. The trouble extends, however, to the whole country.

"Ask parents the cause. The situation is discouraging, and nowhere is it more so than in this city. With thousands of dollars expended, and with children in vast numbers, our church is not getting hold of them. Our failure to do so in this generation will be felt in church membership records in the next."

It has long been said by Protestants: "If we can only get the children we are all right," but even the Sunday School is now failing.

One is likely to form the hasty conclusion that because the Protestant churches are not reaching the people that therefore there are not enough churches; that more should be opened, that none should be closed; in short, that the Protestants are niggardly in their support of churches. My own first impression when I began my inquiry was that New York was underchurched; but I soon came to the conclusion that the city to-day is not only not underchurched, but decidedly *overchurched* —I mean so far as audience rooms for Sunday worship are concerned. I have visited a large number of churches of all denominations during the past year; I have attended morning, afternoon and evening services, and in all that time I have been present at only a comparatively few services at which the church could be said to be even well filled. One of these services was at the church of the Paulist Fathers (Roman Catholic), where at the close of a three weeks' mission there were 2,300 people crowded into a church which seats about 1,900. Another service was at an uptown Christian Science church. Another was a noon Lenten service in Old Trinity. I am speaking here of the ordinary religious services; at Easter, when extraordinary musical programs and beautiful displays of flowers are provided, when it is fashionable to go to church, many of the churches are crowded. On the other hand, I have been at services where the audiences were so painfully small that it was hard to understand how the minister had the heart to go on with his sermon. In one Protestant church on the East Side, one Sunday morning not long ago, I found just fourteen people in the audience including myself. It was a good-sized church, heated for the occasion, with an organist and a choir, besides the clergyman who preached the sermon. One is almost driven to the conclusion sometimes that an endowment is the worst possible possession a church can have; for it makes it unnecessary for the church to report constantly to the people, or to draw its life blood from the people. Not only rich churches like Trinity are paralyzed by their money, but numerous small churches, like the Duane Methodist Church in Hudson Street, and the Emmanuel Baptist Church in Suffolk Street, live a miserable, hopeless existence, spending their income, it is true, but more dead than alive. This does not mean, of course, that there are not plenty of people of all sorts and of every denomination swarming about, but that *these people don't go to church.*

WHAT SHALL THE CHURCH DO?

Why don't they go to church? What shall the church do?

Upon this question of *doing*, the ministry has divided itself roughly into two great classes. One has sought to save the church by strengthening the institution as it is at present; this, indeed, was naturally the first impulse. Many church leaders have been seeking endowments, building more churches and parish houses, preaching more energetically. And like any institutional group under pressure, its position has often been one of denial and opposition. Having no power of prophecy, no triumphant message, it has scat-

THE PROTESTANT CHURCHES

tered its energies in preaching and working *against* various minor evils. Thus we find the united clergy of various cities campaigning with enthusiasm against Sunday baseball, Sunday concerts, vaudeville and moving picture performances—the amusements of the poor.

Now, I am not entering into the question of vaudeville theaters, moving picture shows and the like (no doubt they are bad enough and need to be closely looked after) nor am I even inquiring why the expensive Sunday automobiling, yachting, opera concerts, and golf of the rich are not as evil in their results as the baseball and vaudevilles of the poor—I am merely illustrating this tendency to preach and organize *against* things, instead of preaching and organizing *for* things. If they could do away with Sunday vaudeville, Sunday baseball, Sunday concerts—what next? How would they supply the deficiency? The people won't come to church anyway. About the only time the workingman really feels the church is when the church tries to take away some of his pleasures!

THE SPIRITUAL UNREST

But another group of church leaders have hesitatingly taken quite another course. They have begun to suspect that possibly the churches were wrong—radically wrong—in their spirit and methods. As one minister put it to me directly:

"We discovered that the giving of money was not enough. We had to go deeper."

Another said:

"We are giving up the idea that it is sufficient to get people into a church building and teach them a doctrine. We must do something more."

This feeling that "we must *do* something," that the church must produce works, developed in some instances into a passion for "efficiency." I know churches to-day where the word "efficiency" has become a sort of fetich; and I know more than one worker who is half killing himself with his varied activities. They must at all events *do* something. But what shall they do?

They do not realize that efficiency of itself is nothing, that mere "doing" is nothing. For there can be no real efficiency without vision. Unless a man knows to what end he

THE PROTESTANT CHURCHES

is working, what shall all his arduous days and sleepless nights profit him?

CAN THE CHURCHES GET BACK TO THE PEOPLE?

There has been, indeed, no lack of experimentation during the last ten or fifteen years among a growing group of thoughtful progressives. Though it is difficult to break away from tradition, many Protestant churches have been doing it. It was a decided innovation when men like Rainsford in the Episcopal Church, and Judson among the Baptists, added to their church work such accessories as carpenter shops, gymnasiums, baths, and parlors, and organized all sorts of clubs and classes. It was surely a drastic and original step when men like Worcester in Boston, and Batten in New York, turned their attention to healing sick bodies, as well as sick souls. I shall describe the Emmanuel Movement in a later chapter in this book. In another church, the Church of the Ascension, Mr. Irvine, a Socialist, addresses a large audience every Sunday evening, and a socialistic discussion is held afterward—surely, an unusual activity for the church. Another Episcopal Church,

THE SPIRITUAL UNREST

St. George's, which numbers among its members some of the richest men in New York, holds a revival and the clergymen and the choir, with all the congregation, goes out and marches singing in the streets to gather in the people from the by-ways and hedges.

These unusual new activities are but a few examples of many experiments which the Protestant churches are now trying.

When summed up, all these movements mean just one thing: that the Protestant churches, having fled from the common people, are trying various constructive measures for *getting back to the common people*. They are trying new ways of serving the people, whether with carpenter shops, baths, bodily healing or socialist discussions. And all of them are full of significance. They are signs of that spirit of humility, that willingness to do service, which always accompanies the appearance of new truth. Each contains a fundamentally valuable idea, each is leading men and women toward a new vision of the high place which the church should occupy in our modern life.

When I began this inquiry all these move-

THE PROTESTANT CHURCHES

ments loomed large upon the horizon, for they have had wide secular publicity, and they have been eagerly hailed and enthusiastically commended in certain progressive church circles. But viewing the whole field, as well as studying specific neighborhoods and specific churches, I have been surprised to find how little, after all, the real religious situation has been changed by all the devices so far attempted. In the first place, comparatively few churches among the hundreds in New York, have attempted any of the new work. The majority of the churches are still simply content. Moreover, where the experiments are tried, the same sort of works—clubs, classes, baths, gymnasiums, to say nothing of bodily healing and socialist discussions, are being done and often better done by other agencies—such as the settlements and schools. Some of the churches which made a fine start in institutional work are already finding it difficult to maintain that work with any great enthusiasm. Dr. Batten and other clergymen who with rare energy have been trying the Emmanuel Movement have attracted more people to their churches—but they are practically all Protestants drawn away from other Protestant churches. I say this in no spirit of carping criticism, but merely as a statement of conditions. A small group of people, already socialists, attend and enjoy the addresses and socialist discussions at the Church of the Ascension.

FAILURE OF REVIVALS IN NEW YORK CITY.

As for revivals, although some of the greatest revivalists in the world, men like "Gypsy" Smith and W. J. Dawson, have recently conducted extended services in New York, practically nothing has been accomplished. A few backsliding Protestants have been reached, but, broadly speaking, the situation remains unchanged.

All the new devices, indeed, taken together, have not prevented the steady decline of church influence, nor have they changed, as yet, the tone of disheartenment with which many Protestant leaders look upon the situation. A million or more Protestants are still outside of Protestant church influence, to say nothing of the Roman Catholics and Jewish people. Dr. Worcester of Boston, who has

THE PROTESTANT CHURCHES

had one of the most active institutional churches in the country, strikes a common note of discouragement when he says:

"I have heard many of the ablest and most conscientious clergymen of our church confess with tears that they are doing this work with a sense of despondency and humiliation because they do not feel that they are giving the people the best they have to give.

"In other words, the church of Christ cannot maintain and propagate itself by anything less comprehensive, less spiritual and tremendous than the Christian religion, and the plain truth is we are not bringing the full force of our religion to bear upon the hearts and lives of the people."

In all this work, indeed, there is no resistless or triumphant note of faith. Many of the experiments are timid and soon become apologetic, and in nearly all cases the new movements spring up, not as the common inspiration of a denomination, or even of a single church, but are the result of some individual inspiration. *There is no group impetus*. It was not the Episcopal Church which spoke in the Emmanuel Movement (the Bishop is reported to "tolerate" it), but a single bold-hearted man. A Parkhurst springs into feverish activity and accomplishes results, not because he is a Presbyterian, or because a great church is behind him (a good many church people were against him), but because he is a strong individual, fired with a zeal for social betterment.

The Protestant churches, as churches, may be said, indeed, to have no longer any very positive convictions or any very definite program. No longer fighting one another, neither do they unite; there is no fire to fuse them. A "Federation of Churches" exists in New York, but it is hardly more than the activity of one energetic man whose valuable statistical studies of church conditions have been financed by contributions from various denominations. It has almost no significance as a directing or centralizing power.

I have said that the Protestant churches, having been withdrawing from the common people for a hundred years, are now trying to get back. To this end they have given much money; it has not availed. Neither has charity re-established them, nor mission chap-

THE PROTESTANT CHURCHES

els, nor even carpenter shops, clubs, classes, gymnasiums, socialist discussions, nor revivals.

WHAT IS REALLY THE TROUBLE WITH THE CHURCHES?

What, then, is the trouble?

The Archbishop of Canterbury said recently that he worked seventeen hours a day and had no time left to form an opinion as to the solution of the problem of the unemployed. To which Keir Hardie replied that "a religion which demands seventeen hours a day for organization and leaves nothing for a single thought about starving and despairing men, women and children, has no message for this age."

Two remarkable reports have just been issued, one a study of workingmen's budgets in New York, by Prof. Robert Coit Chapin of Beloit College; another a report of industrial conditions in the city of Pittsburgh by a staff of trained investigators. Both of these reports show conclusively that a very large number of the people in our great cities are chronically overworked and underfed. Many of the families investigated for Professor Chapin's book had incomes so small that it is difficult to believe that human beings could exist on them without outside help. There was also a considerable percentage of actual underfeeding—even among those of higher incomes.

And Dr. Edward T. Devine gives this summary of the findings (in part) of the Pittsburgh survey which will apply with more or less force to conditions of the working class in all American cities:

"An altogether incredible amount of overwork by everybody, reaching its extreme in the twelve-hour shift for seven days in the week in the steel mills and the railway switch yards.

"Low wages for the great majority of the laborers employed by the mills, so low as to be inadequate for the maintenance of a normal American standard of living.

"Still lower wages for women.

"An absentee capitalism, with bad effects strikingly analogous to those of absentee landlordism of which Pittsburgh furnishes noteworthy examples.

"The destruction of family life, not in any imaginary or mystical sense, but by the de-

THE PROTESTANT CHURCHES

mands of the day's work and by the very demonstrable and material method of typhoid fever and industrial accidents, both preventable, but costing in single years in Pittsburgh considerably more than a thousand lives, and irretrievably shattering nearly as many homes."

At the same time that this condition exists among the working people, wealth has been increasing, the "steel magnates," the "railroad kings," the "coal and oil barons," have been growing richer and richer. Along with discomfort in the tenements have grown elaborate luxuries, elaborate amusements in the homes, hotels, and clubs of the rich. Nor need we go to any socialist agitator to draw the conclusions; we have it from the scientific experts of the Pittsburgh survey in these words:

"The contrast, which does not become blurred by familiarity with detail, but, on the contrary, becomes more vivid as the outlines are filled in—the contrast between the prosperity on the one hand of the most prosperous of all the communities of our Western civilization, with its vast natural resources, the generous fostering of government, the human energy, the technical development, the gigantic tonnage of the mines and mills, the enormous capital of which the bank balances afford an indication; and, on the other hand, the neglect of life, of health, of physical vigor, even of the industrial efficiency of the individual.

"Certainly no community before in America or Europe has ever had such a surplus, and never before has a great community applied what it had so meagerly to the rational purposes of human life. Not by gifts of libraries, galleries, technical schools and parks, but by the cessation of toil one day in seven and sixteen hours in the twenty-four, by the increase of wages, by the sparing of lives, by the prevention of accidents, and by raising the standards of domestic life, should the surplus come back to the people of the community in which it is created."

NO MESSAGE FOR THE COMMON PEOPLE.

This is the situation which the Protestant churches are facing. Many of the rich are in the churches; nearly all of the poor are outside. The churches feel that somehow they must "get back to the people." But they

THE PROTESTANT CHURCHES

have not yet touched the real problem. Here and there a man is crying in the wilderness, crying to a people who are spending their wealth on themselves. The churches, as churches, have not waked up. They are still dallying with symptoms; offering classes and gymnasiums to people who are underfed and underpaid, who live in miserable and unsanitary homes! They wonder why revivals of the sort of religion they preach do not attract the multitudes. They devote tremendous energy in attempting to suppress vaudeville shows while hundreds of thousands of women and children in New York are being degraded body and soul by senseless exploitation—too much work, too small wages, poor homes, no amusement. They help the poor child and give no thought to the causes which have made him poor. They have no vision of social justice; they have no message for the common people. They are afraid to face the world "without purse or scrip." And without such vision how shall they reach the hearts of men? Of what purpose is their "passion for efficiency"?

"The world," says the Reverend Dr. Cochran, of Philadelphia, "will not be satisfied with our religious professions until we attack the causes of poverty and disease with the same enthusiasm and persistency that we palliate the symptoms."

NEW YORK OVERCHURCHED BUT UNDERWORKED.

I have said that New York is at present overchurched rather than underchurched; but I might with equal truth say that New York, religiously, is extraordinarily *underworked*. Everywhere I went I heard the same plea:

"If we could only get a few more helpers! What we need is workers."

This I have heard not only among the churches but among settlements, and in all sorts of progressive movements. In short, men and women are wanted everywhere. *Human touch, not money, is required. There must be personal self-sacrifice.* It was not until Francis of Assisi stripped himself naked that "he won for himself a secret sympathy in many souls."

At first when Francis of Assisi renounced the world and sought to follow his Lady of Poverty, the people said he was assuredly mad. He could not wholly convince the

THE PROTESTANT CHURCHES

people of his sincerity, for he had been a rich young man. The Bishop finally advised Francis to give up all his property.

"To the great surprise of the crowd, Francis, instead of replying, retired to a room in the Bishop's palace, and immediately reappeared absolutely naked, holding in his hand the packet into which he had rolled his clothes; these he laid down before the Bishop with the little money that he still had kept, saying: 'Listen, all of you, and understand it well; until this time I have called Pictro Bernardone my father, but now I desire to serve God. This is why I return to him this money, for which he has given himself so much trouble, as well as my clothing, and all that I have had from him, for from henceforth I desire to say nothing else than Our Father, who art in Heaven.'"

Of this act the chronicle says: "On that day he won for himself a secret sympathy in many souls." And in a few years all Italy was at his feet.

The churches to-day are still far more interested in having fine buildings, in being Baptists, or Presbyterians, or Lutherans, than

THE SPIRITUAL UNREST

they are in reaching the people. They make no real surrender. A complaint has gone up from the churches for several years of a lack of young men entering the ministry; it is laid down as a reason that ministers are not paid enough salary. But that is not the true reason: the true reason is that young men of ideals feel little inspiration or vision within the churches. The churches offer them no great message to deliver. Men who are willing to sacrifice most, never do it for salaries. And there is never any lack of men to go through fire and tempt death if only they are aflame with a great purpose.

Can the Protestant churches, divided among themselves, full of the pride of tradition, and rich in worldly possessions, ever rise to the situation?

CHAPTER III

THE DISINTEGRATION OF THE JEWS—
A STUDY OF THE SYNAGOGUE

IN former chapters I have considered the state of the Protestant church, especially in New York City. The next greatest element of population in the metropolis is the Jew. Let us consider how he has been faring religiously.

When I went down into the swarming East Side of New York City, I began to understand what a Christian minister meant when he referred to the "stone-wall of Judaism." I found the few Protestant churches which still remained, in a distressing state of decay—dying out, withering down, like trees in barren soil. When I inquired for reasons the ministers and missionaries had many things to tell me, but they usually summed up their explanation with the remark that the presence of the Jew was fatal to Christian churches.

THE SPIRITUAL UNREST

How much the Jewish population means in the life of New York City, few people realize. Within the past few years, quietly, almost without notice, the Jew has become the chief single element in the population of our principal American city—and in a very real sense one of the dominating factors of our life. Out of the total population of Greater New York nearly 1,000,000 are Jews, or more than one in every five. Nowhere at any time in the world's history were so many Jews gathered together in one locality. Jerusalem the Golden in all the 5,000 years of its history never had a quarter as many Jews as now live in New York City, and all Palestine to-day, in spite of the efforts of enthusiastic Zionists to fire their people with a desire to return to their home land, has not as many Jewish residents as may be found in half a dozen blocks on the East Side. Not only are they the dominant factor on the crowded East Side, but they occupy whole neighborhoods in other parts of the city—in Harlem and the Bronx, in Williamsburg and Brownsville—almost to the exclusion of other population. And they are not mere renters of homes and tenements; for a considerable pro-

DISINTEGRATION OF THE JEWS

portion of the valuable land on Manhattan Island is now held by Jewish owners. The largest single industry in the city—clothing manufacture—is almost wholly in the hands of Jews. They control many of our greatest banks and other financial institutions, and their power in finance is rapidly extending; they dominate and direct almost exclusively the amusements, both theaters and operas—of the greatest American city. About half of the principal newspapers of the metropolis are owned by Jews—and some of the other papers have Jewish editors in important positions. They control the greater part of the wholesale and retail trade. Many of our ablest lawyers, doctors and scientists are Jews. More and more the Jew is becoming a great factor in politics.

Many Jewish judges now administer our laws, and not a few Jews in our legislatures and in Congress are helping to make them. The education of the children of New York City is, to a surprising extent, in the hands of the Jews—and becoming more and more so. I examined the lists recently published of newly appointed teachers for the public schools. It reads for long spaces like a directory of the East Side. Hundreds of teachers in New York who were born in despotic Russia and who came here only a few years ago, knowing not a word of English, are to-day teaching American children the principles of democracy. Some of the strongest benevolent and civic activities of the city are controlled by Jews and, finally, the Jews, resisting Christianity, have built up at least one religious or ethical movement which has attracted many Christians. Not a few Christian churches, slowly surrounded by Jews, have given up the struggle and their buildings have finally been purchased and converted into synagogues. It may come as a surprise to many people, but it is a fact that there are now far more synagogues (organizations, not buildings) on Manhattan Island than there are Christian churches. The number of Jewish synagogues in Greater New York is 803, of which 708 are in Manhattan Island and the Bronx. Assuredly New York City has become the New Jerusalem of the Jew. And not in the Ghetto only, but throughout all strata of the common life.

DISINTEGRATION OF THE JEWS

JEWISH IDEALS AND AMERICAN LIFE.

It would make a study of profound interest to determine how far the Jew and Jewish ideals are modifying in essential particulars the life and thought of American cities. We are accustomed, in our self-assurance, to regard the Jew either as an interloper to be superciliously set apart and kept apart, or else as an alien to be assimilated and made Christian as rapidly as possible. We imagine with a swelling of our pride that we are making over all these Jews and other foreigners to our ideas of what an American should be; we forget that we are also being made over to *their* ideas of what an American should be. With the Jew so largely dominating the three greatest engines of popular opinion and popular education—the schools, the public press, and the stage—it would certainly be astonishing if the life and ideals of the city were not vitally modified.

I do not mean to say that the Jews are consciously trying to change our life or that they do not become loyal and patriotic Americans. But civilization is a sort of pudding, changed to the taste by every added ingredient. With a million Jews in our metropolitan pudding, the conduct of our business, our religious observances, our ideas of art and music, cannot fail to be essentially modified.

From the time of Jesus down, the church has labored with greater persistence and less success to convert the Jews than any other people. At times it has pursued Mahomet's policy of "the sword or the faith," and by force and persecution has brought a few Jews into the church; at other times it has used the velvet hand of persuasion. Both methods are still in vogue, the method of force being in these latter days in America thinly veiled under forms of prejudice, ostracism, and the lesser sorts of persecution. As for the method of persuasion, it was probably never employed more widely than it is to-day. Within the last ten years the Christian churches of America have awakened as never before to the so-called Jewish problem. They want now to break down the "stone wall of the Jew" which has been building for so many centuries at the hands of Christian governments. And they find the wall curiously defended on the other side!

DISINTEGRATION OF THE JEWS

"After persecuting us for a thousand years and more in the name of Christ, you come to us and ask us to believe in that Christ!" exclaims the Jew.

EFFORTS TO PROSELYTE THE JEWS.

I have visited, at various times, quite a number of these missions to the Jews, and all of them without exception have impressed me with the discouraging feebleness of their work. Most of the leaders in Jewish missions, those who know most of conditions, frankly express their discouragement. They work very hard indeed for meager results. A few hundred conversions are reported every year, but after a century of activity, the total Jewish membership in evangelical Christian churches, according to a careful investigation made by an ardent supporter of Hebrew missions, the Rev. Louis Meyer of the Presbyterian Church, is less than 10,000, including children, out of a total Jewish population of 2,000,000. And this is counterbalanced in some degree by Christians who have joined the Jewish synagogues, of whom there is no inconsiderable number. Although the Jews never invite proselytes, I know one synagogue in New York which receives about ten Christians a year, mostly Christian wives of Jewish men.

Among the great mass of Jews in the country, the Christian missions have not stirred the least interest. In fact, I found from many inquiries among all sorts of Jews that the prevailing attitude was one of indifference or of contempt. Only in a few instances have the missions succeeded even in arousing the tribute of open hostility. Their fear of Christianity is of a very different sort, as I shall show.

Thus, in spite of persecution, in spite of determined missionary efforts, the Jew has steadily gone on increasing in numbers until to-day there is a larger Jewish population in the world than ever before. It was only a handful of Jews that Moses led out of Egypt, compared with the 12,000,000 now scattered abroad among the nations.

But let us look more deeply into the condition of the Jews. The "stone wall of Judaism" is by no means as high or as strong as a superficial examination would indicate.

DISINTEGRATION OF THE JEWS

It is, in fact, nothing more than a scenery wall —painted paper—with a Hebrew inscription which no Christian and comparatively few American Jews can read. And that inscription is the closing words of the Passover prayer: "And next year may we be in Zion." Behind the wall, among themselves, the Jews are engaged in a heated discussion as to what is meant by "Zion"—Jerusalem or New York!

UNREST AMONG THE JEWS.

When I began to make inquiries among the Jews, themselves—in three different cities, New York, Boston and Chicago—I discovered an extraordinary condition of upheaval and unrest. It is one of the commonest of human errors to imagine that a distant people are all, somehow, exactly like one another, and at the same time very different from ourselves. But when we become really acquainted with those distant people we find them curiously human like ourselves, swept by the same interests and hopes and fears, divided by the same issues, concerned with the same problems.

And so the Jews. As I talked with Jewish

religious leaders I had often to remind myself that I was not talking with Christian ministers, so similar were the stories told and the complaints made of the decline of religious interest. I heard the same lament that religion no longer influenced men's lives, that the synagogues, although very numerous, were illy-attended and poorly supported, that home-worship, a central feature of the Jewish religion, was falling into decay, and finally, one rabbi, when I asked him what was the trouble with the Jewish religion, answered me in two words: "Your Christianity."

Though he did not mean by Christianity quite what the word means to most of us, this remark contained a world of significance, as I shall show.

Thus, strangely enough, I found the Christian church on the one hand giving the Jew as a reason for its decline in certain localities, and the Jew responding with the assertion that Christianity was one of the causes for the disintegration of his religion. As a matter of fact, the cause lies deeper than either thinks, and it is the same in both cases. A worldwide liberalism is shaking ancient institutions;

DISINTEGRATION OF THE JEWS

old walls are everywhere tottering. The Roman Catholic has his Modernist, the Protestant his Higher Critic, and the Jew his Reform Movement. It goes deep—this spiritual unrest.

And nowhere deeper than among the Jews, whose intellectual faculties have been sharpened for centuries upon the gritty texts of the Old Testament and the Talmud. It is scarcely necessary to recall the fact that many of the ideas which are now most deeply stirring mankind are the product of thinkers who were Jews. The beginning of the socialist movement traces back to two Jews, Marx and Lasalle; the peace movement had its inspiration in a book by Jean de Bloch, a Jew; and the ethical culture movement in America, the length and breadth of which is not yet appreciated, is largely the inspiration of Dr. Felix Adler, a Jew. The Jewish people have always possessed the genius for declaring revolutionary truths, for prophecy. We sometimes forget that modern civilization rests largely upon Jewish prophecy and Jewish law-giving, Moses and David and Isaiah, Jesus and Paul—all Jews.

THE SPIRITUAL UNREST

JEWISH ORTHODOXY IN NEW YORK.

Before we can understand what a liberal movement signifies, we must form a clear conception of the orthodoxy from which it is a revolt.

In Grand Street, the Broadway of the East Side, you will recognize instantly the common type of the orthodox Jew. He looks very much as he looked when he walked the dirty streets of his native Russian or Austrian village. His black coat, his long black beard, his rounded shoulders, the Hebrew curls at his temples, indelibly mark his place in the heterogeneous life of the streets. He can be seen walking with serene countenance in the midst of this seething caldron of modern life as unscathed as Shadrach, Meshach and Abednego in the fiery furnace of King Nebuchadnezzar, and with as profound a faith in the watchfulness of a personal God.

He came here, this serene old Jew, four thousand miles from Eastern Europe, and about five hundred years from the Middle Ages. In Russia, Austria or Roumania, he lived mostly in small towns, set apart and much forced upon himself. He knew little of modern learning, modern science or modern industry, but he was deeply versed in the wisdom of old religious books. Though dwelling in an age of nationalism which is already dreaming of universalism, he remained in what was essentially a tribal stage of civilization with a tribal God, and a tribal conception of religion. In a real sense his religion commanded every act of his life in a way that we can scarcely realize. The synagogue to the Jew in Russia is very much what the Middle Ages' cathedral was to the Roman Catholic, or as the Protestant church was to the Puritans of New England—the center of his life.

When the Jew reaches New York he brings his tribal instincts and his tribal conception of God with him, and the first thing he does is to attempt to set up and continue his tribal institutions. He does not know it, of course, but the source of liberalism—indeed, of revolution, if the spirit of liberalism be long repressed—is the attempt to apply fifteenth or even nineteenth century institutions, unchanged, to twentieth century conditions.

THE SPIRITUAL UNREST

Orthodoxy never seems to learn that anything grows!

EAST SIDE SYNAGOGUES.

In its ecclesiastical institutions no religion is freer or more democratic than the Jewish. Among the Jews there is no authority comparable to the Roman Catholic Pope, no denominational supervision, no ordained clergy. Any ten Jews may organize a synagogue, elect a president, and choose one of their number as a reader, or employ a rabbi. This accounts for the very large number of Jewish synagogical congregations in New York City. Each is made up largely of men from the same town in Russia, or of the same district in Austria. Only a comparatively few of the older and larger congregations—like that composed of Jews from Krakow, Austria— have buildings of their own. A few have bought out and rearranged abandoned Christian churches, but the great majority of the synagogues are mere rented rooms in tenement houses or sometimes halls or lofts. I have visited a single tenement on the East Side with three different synagogues in it. In one

DISINTEGRATION OF THE JEWS

building in Ridge Street I found a store on the first floor, a sweat-shop on the second floor (with families living in the rear), two synagogues on the third and fourth floors and then another sweat-shop at the top. It costs only fifty or seventy-five dollars for a scroll of the law (written on sheepskin by scribes in Russia), which is the main requisite of a synagogue; the members themselves often do the necessary carpentering, and the women make the altar curtains. A few seats for the men, a little shut-in, stuffy gallery for the women, and an altar toward Jerusalem—and the synagogue is complete.

Eagerly the incoming Jew attends his little synagogue. For a time it is almost as much a center of his life as it was in Russia. He gathers there with his neighbors morning, noon and night, discussing not only religious but secular affairs of all sorts. Sometimes he opens a little school or *chedar* in which his children learn the Hebrew prayers; sometimes he allows poorer Jews to sleep there at night; and sometimes the temple is even put to more mundane uses. In one synagogue in a dingy back alley I saw an old oilcloth merchant arranging his wares among the pews. For a time, also, the Jew is scrupulous in his observances of dietary laws and of all other rites and ceremonies. Every morning he binds his phylacteries (little leather boxes containing passages of the scripture) to his arm and forehead while he prays, and he is particular to wear, under his clothing, the sacred "four corners" or "fringes." We may smile as we will at the droning, swaying worshipers, "gabbling their prayers," as Zangwill says, in the little East Side synagogues, it is still a fact that many of these blackbearded orthodox Jews practice a severity of morality not so common in this age as to be despised.

There is, indeed, something infinitely pathetic in the effort of these old Jews to maintain their religion in New York; and in less exaggerated form, one may see the older Presbyterians, Methodists and Roman Catholics struggling desperately in the torrent of modern progress to preserve all the old customs and traditions of their churches. And yet these intensely earnest older Jews are engaged in the ancient, unseeing task of trying to crowd an expanding and exuberant universe into their own little, institutional pint cups. The Jew finds himself in a life inconceivably broader, freer, swifter than anything he knew in Russia. Most of the older men and women, indeed, never get into the current of the new life at all; but the moment the young people secure work and begin to learn the English language, they are irresistibly swept away from the old religious moorings. Philip Davis, a Russian Jew, who came here a youth, began in a sweat-shop, graduated at Harvard University, and is now in public work in Boston, says of his experiences:

STORY OF A RUSSIAN JEW.

"For the first six months my religious convictions were unshaken. Somehow I could find no work and therefore had ample time to take in even more than three divine daily services, if need be. But at last I got work in one of the old-time sweat-shops of New York, first as a basting-puller, then as a half-baster. From the moment I entered the shop my religious interest began to decline. In a year it was practically *nil*. My 'four corners' wore out and were never replaced; my fore-

THE SPIRITUAL UNREST

locks disappeared; my phylacteries and my prayer-book were in exile. I ceased going to the synagogue, first only on week days, later on Saturdays as well. In after years I never entered it but twice a year, at the anniversary of my mother's death and during the day of atonement."

DECLINE OF THE SYNAGOGUE.

I have had much to say of the decline of church attendance, but the same tendency is observable among the synagogues. I have visited many of them on Friday evenings and Saturday mornings—the two principal services of the week. Often I have found half a dozen bearded men waiting there—for what reason at first I could not understand. They would look up hopefully when I came in, and then their faces would fall when they saw that I was a Gentile and therefore would not help to make up the necessary prayer-quorum of ten, without which they could not begin their services. Sometimes one of the number will go out on the street and beseech passing Jews to come in and help them with their quorum.

DISINTEGRATION OF THE JEWS

I never shall forget one of these old Jews—his wistful eyes, his gentle, ineffectual movements—whom I saw one day stepping out like some patriarch from his fifteenth century synagogue and seeking to stop with a call to prayer, the tide of the twentieth century as it rushed through the streets. But some of the more prosperous synagogues, adopting modern methods to solve the problem, have employed a certain number of men to be constantly upon call for making up their prayer-quorums. Even in the largest East Side synagogues the attendance is often pitifully small; I have attended services where there were only twelve or fifteen men, including the cantor, with two or three women in the gallery.

Twice a year the synagogues are crowded—at the great Jewish religious feasts, the Day of Atonement and the New Year. Indeed, hundreds of temporary synagogues are instituted in halls and theaters to accommodate the throng of Jews who renew, upon these solemn occasions, their religious connections. Even the Jews who have lost all their religious faith, who no longer observe the ceremonial laws, will return to the synagogue for the Day of Atonement. In a similar way Christian churches are crowded at Easter, or for the Christmas celebration.

If it were not for the older people and for the constant inflow of immigrants, I don't know what would become of the orthodox religious institutions of the Jews. Not only are the younger people soon alienated from the synagogue by American influences, but of recent years many young people are in secret rebellion against the old religion before they come here. In the last ten years great changes have been taking place in Russia and Austria. Even the Ghetto of the Jew has been penetrated to some extent by modern learning and modern ideas. In talking with Jews I don't know how often I have been told that they were "emancipated" before they came here as a result of reading Russian or German books. One of the ablest Jews in New York told me how he toiled with painful secrecy through a Russian text-book of geography.

"I found," he said, "that the earth revolved

DISINTEGRATION OF THE JEWS

around the sun, not the sun around the earth, as the Talmud had it, and from that moment my faith in the old teachings was broken."

AMERICANIZING OF THE JEWS.

Not only do the younger Jews desert their religious practices, but they often adopt English names, refuse to speak Yiddish and diligently absorb American ideas and customs. It is difficult for us who have always lived in America to realize what a comparatively free country means to a Russian Jew—a country where a man is free to organize, free to say what he thinks and believe what he will, where even citizenship is free. At once his life, formerly centered in the synagogue, finds a hundred new activities to occupy it. The public school is so far better than the dingy, unsanitary, unpedagogical *chedar* where only Hebrew is taught, that it speedily swallows up all the children. Hundreds, indeed, of the little Hebrew *chedarim* are still maintained by the contributions of pious parents, and many children are compelled to go to them after public school hours, but they go under compulsion and stop as soon as possible.

THE SPIRITUAL UNREST

The right of free association has resulted in labor organizations and innumerable societies for every conceivable purpose, many of which draw the Jews from the synagogue. One evening I visited the strike headquarters of an East Side labor union; it was thronged with men—while the nearby synagogue, although it was the prayer-hour, was practically deserted. The young Jews also join the settlement-clubs, they meet in the free parks, they literally swallow the books at the free libraries, they patronize the free city baths to the loss of the innumerable little Jewish bath houses and, wonder of wonders, the Jew who has never known anything of physical culture, takes with avidity to the free gymnasium! As he gets farther away he even joins the Y. M. C. A.—for its non-religious advantages.

It is not long before the Jew begins to break the Sabbath—for in America the pressure of industry and business all tend, and almost irresistibly, to prevent the Jew from observing a different day from the Christian. I have visited the East Side frequently on

Saturday and I have been surprised to see how many of the Jewish stores remain open, how many pushcart men continue to ply their trade even in this heart and center of orthodox Jewry. And breaking away from the Sabbath, neither does the Jew observe the Christian Sunday—at least until he becomes well-to-do and moves up town.

COMMERCIALIZATION OF THE SYNAGOGUE.

In some cases the synagogue itself has become more or less commercialized. A group of men organize a death benefit, or a burial association, or even a sick benefit society, sometimes all three, and a synagogue is maintained as a sort of appendage. It costs little to run, and, indeed, it sometimes makes its members a profit through the sale of seats at high prices during the Jewish feast days. I talked with the president of a somewhat typical East Side orthodox synagogue, a physician interested in many Jewish organizations. He told me very frankly that he himself was a free-thinker, but he thought it well to keep up the synagogue.

"Many of the old people like it," he said, "and it furnishes a place for us to get together."

Of the one hundred and forty members of his synagogue he told me that twenty were "truly religious," about twenty were "halfway religious," and that the other hundred were more or less free-thinkers.

DIETARY LAWS.

I asked a young Russian Jew recently married whether he still observed the dietary laws. This is what he said:

"In a way, yes. We don't make much of the details like keeping the butter and meat dishes apart, but we do eat kosher food. If we didn't the old folks would not come to visit us. We shall keep it up as long as they live."

Many Jews I talked with had much the same thing to say; they did not wish to sadden their parents, so they kept on with a portion, at least, of the forms and ceremonies. They are like thousands of unchurched Christians who to-day go back to a religious institution to be married, have a minister officiate at

DISINTEGRATION OF THE JEWS

funerals, and though their children are not baptized, still send them to Sunday School. Such nominal Christians also celebrate Easter and Christmas as holidays, but with little thought of the significance of these festivals.

The most prevalent attitude toward religion even among the radical Jews is not violent enough to be called atheism; it is rather, as among Christians, one of indifference. A careful investigation made recently by the Federation of Churches of a large district in Harlem occupied chiefly by Jews showed that over eighty per cent. of the Jews acknowledged no connection with any synagogue. As Rabbi Harris said to me:

"The Jew has always survived persecution; will he be able now to survive emancipation?"

EFFORT TOWARD NEW FORMS OF RELIGIOUS EXPRESSION.

Having thus endeavored to show how the old forms of Judaism are breaking up, I come now to the consideration of the experiments which Jews are making toward new forms of religious expression. Men cannot long survive without some form of religion; and if the old breaks down, there is an eager, persistent, indefatigable search for the new.

The present tendency of our civilization might be characterized as one of frank examination; Christians and Jews alike are in a critical mood; we deny the old dogmas of religion, we criticise government, we are dissatisfied with the present methods of industry. The great mass of the people are passive and drifting—waiting for the clear call of new leaders.

Thus the great mass of the Jews, having gone out of the synagogue have gone into nothing else. It is easy to drift, hard to take a positive step into new and unknown enterprises.

One would think, indeed, that this was just the opportunity for the Christian to convert the Jew; but the Christian is in exactly the same state as the Jew. He can't convert the Jew because the Jew cannot see that the Christian applies his doctrines to his own life! Wherever there is reality of faith, the Jew is attracted exactly like any other person. One of the most interesting facts that came to my notice in New York was the growing number of Jews in Christian Science churches. Some of them go into the Christian Science work and still maintain connection with a synagogue. There are even three Jewish Christian Science practitioners on the orthodox East Side. A patient of one of them, asked by a friend of mine what the Christian Scientist told him to do, replied:

"Why, he told me just what the rabbi does, to believe in God."

INFLUENCE OF CHRISTIANITY ON JUDAISM.

In the earlier part of this chapter I spoke of the failure of Christian missions among the Jews, but intimated that the influence of Christianity upon the Jews was none the less profound. It is a curious thing how much farther a little of the practiced Christian Spirit will go than much preaching of the Christian doctrines. Though few Jews come into the churches from the missions, a good many drift in as a result of kindly human association with Christians. Thus many Jews, especially in smaller towns and cities, have been drifting into the churches. Jenkin Lloyd Jones, a Unitarian of Chicago, has a considerable number of Jews in his congregation. When I was in the South two or three years ago studying the Negro problem, I met a number of men with Jewish names, who, by long contact with Christians and isolation from their kind, had drifted into the churches. During the Civil War the Jews of the South were loyal to its cause, and fought shoulder to shoulder with their Gentile brothers. This broke down the wall of prejudice and their children are naturally in the Sunday Schools and become church members as they grow up. Breaking away from forms and seeking the true spirit of religion, Christian and Jew find themselves not far apart, after all.

But the religious drift of the Jew, however much it may be influenced by Christianity, is distinctly not toward the churches as they are now constituted. Why should it be, when Christians themselves are drifting away from their own churches?

Modern Jewry in America may be divided into three great classes. First, the orthodox Jews, made up largely, as I have shown, of the new immigrants on the East Side; second, the indifferent or drifting Jews, who compose a

DISINTEGRATION OF THE JEWS

very large part of the population; third, the Reform Jews, who have taken the positive step to new things.

THE REFORM MOVEMENT.

All the larger and wealthier synagogues, with few exceptions, belong to the Reform group; the Americanized Jew, if he keeps up his religious observances at all, broadly speaking, belongs to a Reform synagogue.

Briefly described, the Reform movement, which began years ago in Germany, is an attempt, like that of modernism among the Roman Catholics, and the social movement among the Protestants, to bring religious institutions up to date.

"The Reform movement," said Rabbi Harris of Temple Israel of New York, "seeks to get at the living essentials of the Jewish faith and apply them to life as it is to-day."

Most of the Reform synagogues that I have visited are far nearer, in their services, to the Protestant churches than they are to the orthodox synagogues. They have sloughed off a large part of the old ceremonies and ritual. A new union prayer-book has been adopted by the Central Conference of American Rabbis, composed of one hundred and eighty-three of the principal Reform congregations in the United States. It is much briefer than the old and contains more English than Hebrew. In the Reform synagogues women have been raised to an equality with men. Instead of being relegated to the gallery—a remnant of Orientalism in the orthodox synagogues—they occupy pews with the men. Music and mixed choirs have been introduced and the preaching is commonly English. Men do not wear their hats in the Reform synagogues according to the ages-old custom among the orthodox Jews. Marriage and burial ceremonies have been simplified and even in some Reform synagogues the great festivals have been shortened. Reform Jews do not observe the ancient dietary laws; indeed, often do not know what they are.

In still more essential ways, however, the Jewish religion has been changed. The orthodox Jew still looks to a miraculous coming of the Messiah, and a physical return of all Jews to Jerusalem. The Reform Jew believes not in miracles but in evolution, and he looks forward to the coming of a Messianic era rather than a personal Messiah. He desires a Zion in which all men will accept the one God, and he believes that the Jews have a mission in bringing about that result. For a belief in the resurrection of the body, he has substituted a belief in the immortality of the soul. He is also much more friendly in receiving proselytes than the orthodox Jew; nor does he require of them the rite of circumcision.

DIFFERENCES AMONG REFORMED JEWS.

In thus describing the Reform movement I have had to speak in the broadest terms, because among Reformers themselves there exists to-day every variety of belief and every stage of ceremonial usage from mild orthodoxy up to extreme radicalism. For example, in Dr. Grossman's synagogue in New York, the men still wear their hats at service—but they use an organ and a mixed choir, and women and men sit together; while in Dr. Silverman's Temple Emanu-El, the most notable of New York synagogues, the men do not wear their hats and services are held on both Saturday and Sunday.

At the extreme radical wing of the Reform Movement stand two remarkable men, Dr. Emil G. Hirsch, of Sinai Temple of Chicago, who is the greatest leader of liberal Judaism in this country, and Dr. Stephen S. Wise, who organized two years ago, the Free Synagogue in New York. Both of these men are brilliant and effective speakers and their utterances upon public questions have been marked with singular courage. Both have given up entirely the Friday and Saturday services— the last stronghold of Judaism—and hold their services on Sunday; and both, in common with most Reform synagogues, have adopted the Christian idea of Sunday and Bible schools to teach the English Bible. But most significant of all, perhaps, both have taken exactly the same steps that the more progressive Christian churches have taken, and have started extensive institutional activities.

The idea of a gymnasium, secular clubs and manual training in connection with a synagogue is utterly inconceivable, of course, to the orthodox Jew.

"They give lessons in carpentry and teach men to box with gloves," an orthodox rabbi told me with distress; "they have forgotten the law; they eat unclean food."

Not only have Dr. Hirsch and Dr. Wisc instituted extended institutional features, but other leaders, like Dr. Gries of Cleveland, who has a highly successful work, Dr. Harris of New York, and many others, have made noteworthy progress in the same direction.

JEWISH INTEREST IN JESUS.

One of the curious and interesting things about the progressive Jew is his interest in Jesus, and his changing attitude toward Jesus. Among orthodox Jews, as they come to this country, the name of Jesus is execrated, and his name is even coupled with ribald and disgusting stories. While no Jew acknowledges the deity of Jesus, or admits that he was in truth the Messiah, many of them look upon him with pride as one of the great Jewish prophets. It is not at all unusual in the more liberal synagogues to hear the speaker quote from the New Testament, or speak of Jesus.

"The Jew, of whatever shade of opinion," said Dr. Hirsch in one of his discourses, "is willing to acknowledge the charm, the beauty, the whole-souled perfection of the great prophet of Nazareth. He belongs to us. . . . But all of us are also agreed in this; that what he taught was not a revelation new to the synagogues; for neither in his morality nor in his religious hope did he advance one step beyond the teachings of contemporaneous Judaism. . . . But as a matter of expression, putting the matter so as to vest it with the force of almost a new thought, Jesus commands a place among the few chosen of God."

Dr. Hirsch concludes his discourse in these remarkable words:

"If Jesus were to come back to earth today, the Christians would not admit him to their clubs because he is a Jew; if St. Paul were to come to life he would not be received; St. Peter would not be allowed as a guest at a summer hotel, because, forsooth he is a Hebrew. And therefore the synagogue must

DISINTEGRATION OF THE JEWS

continue to exist if for no other reason than to give Jesus a home."

In short, the faith of the Reform Jew is almost identical with that of the Unitarian, and his methods of work can scarcely be distinguished from those of the more advanced Protestant churches. Dr. Hirsch once replied wittily when asked if he were not really a Unitarian:

"No, I am a Jewnitarian."

ETHICAL CULTURE MOVEMENT.

Still beyond Reform Judaism, dispensing wholly with theology, is the Ethical Culture Movement, the originator of which was Dr. Felix Adler, a Jew, which has attracted to its support many Jews and not a few Christians. The essence of the movement is expressed in its motto, "Deed, not Creed"; the extreme application of the doctrine of works as contrasted with faith. One of its aims is "to teach that the moral law has an immediate authority not contingent on the truth of religious belief, or of philosophical theories."

Of course, all this progressive movement,

supported as it is by the wealthiest Jews, having its own religious schools and colleges, has not gone forward without producing back eddies and revulsions of feeling. Most men are temperamentally conservative; they fear the new step; truth for them must be well buttressed with traditions, else it is no truth. The ruthless sweeping away of ancient ceremonial, and, more than anything else, the de-Judaizing of Jews under the influence of Americanism, has alarmed many conservative Jews. Rabbi Asher said recently in an interview:

"Americanism means becoming completely secularized and thoroughly de-Judaized in every way. There is not a single Jew in Fifth Avenue who will keep his Sabbath."

Moreover, this little group of cultivated orthodox leaders, who are crying for a return to the old customs, look with terror on what Dr. Asher calls "the disorder, the lawlessness, the lewdness of the children" of the second generation. For freedom, and the sudden removal of restraint, which on the one hand has enabled Jews to attain distinction in all branches of American life, has, at the other

DISINTEGRATION OF THE JEWS

extreme, resulted in the wholesale wreckage of the lives of many young Jews. The awful cost of swift progress of the jump from the fifteenth to the twentieth century, is seen in the numbers of Jews arrested for crime or confined in our penal institutions. Sudden freedom is both a wonderful and a dangerous thing!

"When once the Jew breaks away," a highly cultivated orthodox Jew said to me, "where can he stop? The path of the reformer is toward more reform; can he halt this side of a Godless Ethical Culture Movement on the one hand, or a perfunctory Christianity on the other?"

THE REACTION TOWARD ORTHODOXY.

To meet this situation a Jewish Theological Seminary has been established in New York to train orthodox rabbis. One of the greatest of living Hebrew scholars—Dr. Solomon Schechter—is its president. And yet, though it has been in existence now for a number of years it has only twenty-four students in the rabbinical course, with two graduates last year. Jacob H. Schiff, though himself a Reform Jew, has been one of the chief contributors to the work. Orthodox schools on the East Side have also been assisted, but so far very little has been accomplished.

Another movement which is in part a protest against the disintegration of the Jews, and in part a struggle to escape at last from persecution, is Zionism. But even Zionism partakes of the present world-longing for reality, for reducing faith to works. For centuries the Jews have been longing and expecting to return to Palestine; and now, though Zionism has no hold among Reform Jews, there is a desire even among many who are religious free thinkers to make Zion an actuality. Thousands of Jews in America are annually paying their shekel to the Zionist Societies, some are investing in land in Palestine, and a few, a very few, go there every year. But to the vast proportion of Jews Zionism means nothing.

At a recent conference of American Rabbis (the Reform body), a declaration was made that "America is the Jews' Jerusalem and Washington their Zion."

Most of the Reform synagogues are made

DISINTEGRATION OF THE JEWS

up chiefly of German Jews. Few of the Russians, Austrians and Roumanians who came later than the Germans, and who now make up the great bulk of the Jewish population in America, have gone into the Reform Movement. They express their liberalism more in the form of Socialism. Many of the Jews of the East Side are strongly inclined toward Socialism. The chief leaders of Socialism in New York, men like Abraham Cahan, Morris Hillquit, and others, are all Jews.

FUNDAMENTAL NOTE IN THE NEW JEWISH LIBERALISM.

Thus the social idea—the religion of brotherhood among men—whether it expresses itself in the institutional synagogues and charities of the richer Reform Jew, in the Socialism of the Russian Jew, or in the teachings of duty by the Ethical Culture Society, is the predominant note in the new Jewish liberalism, as it is in Christianity. Profoundly fundamental has always been the social teaching of Judaism; the duty of man to man. The Hebrew prophecies are full of Socialism.

And the situation of the Jew for centuries, cut off from the larger world, persecuted and proscribed, has developed a rare spirit of mutual helpfulness. Attention need scarcely be called to the charities of the Jew. He has always cared for his own poor, and to-day in every American city his charitable organizations of all sorts are of the best. Men like Jacob H. Schiff of New York, who is almost a charitable institution in himself, Julius Rosenwald, "the Jacob Schiff of Chicago," Judge Sulzberger of Philadelphia, have not only given with a prodigal hand but have devoted much of their time to the organization of charitable enterprises.

And with the socialization of religion, among Jews as among Christians, comes a widening of the sense of social responsibility toward all mankind. Thus we find many leading Jews not only interested in helping their own people, but in forwarding every sort of good cause—working hand in hand with progressive Christians. Among leaders of reform and civic activities in every part of the country are to be found Jews; Filene and Brandeis of Boston; Schiff of New York;

DISINTEGRATION OF THE JEWS

Lessing Rosenthal, Judge Julian W. Mack and others in Chicago.

No one can study the religious tendencies among the Jews without discovering how closely they resemble the progressive movements among Christians. Both Christians and Jews are moving silently but irresistibly toward the same goal. The Jew will never come into the church as it is now constituted; neither will the Christian become a Jew, but both are rapidly coming together upon the vital, fundamental truths which underlie both religions. For Truth, if it be Truth, cannot be different for Christians than for Jews—no matter how varied the temporary expression of it in creed, or ritual, or ceremonial.

PART II

CHAPTER IV

THE SLUM MISSION AND THE INSTITUTIONAL CHURCH: A COMPARISON OF THEIR FUNCTIONS

HAVING considered, in the three former chapters, the condition of the churches and synagogues, I shall give in succeeding chapters an account of some of the ways in which the churches are seeking to meet the conditions which now confront them, especially in the large cities.

Two things the church has to do—no more, no less. One is to inspire the individual man with faith in God, the other is to draw all men together in a more friendly and democratic relationship. The old formula, love of God, love of fellowmen, expresses the whole range of the activities of the church. Some religious institutions like the Jerry McAuley Mission, emphasize individual regenera-

THE SLUM MISSION

tion, others, like Christ Church of New York City, emphasize social reconstruction. The two types are presented here in contrast; the one lifts men individually out of the gutter, the other also seeks to remove the gutter. Which is the more necessary?

The McAuley Mission is in Water Street below the Bowery, and almost underneath the huge Manhattan end of the old Brooklyn Bridge. The immediate neighborhood, which at one time was one of the very worst on Manhattan Island, has now been partially built up to warehouses, but not far away are still to be found the poorest sort of poor homes and some of the worst of saloons. When the churches began their flight northward years ago, deserting the poorer people, this part of the city was left the prey to every devil of the slums. It was a district without religion, without even humanity. Dozens of saloons and dives were to be found in every block. Kit Burns's famous "rat-pit" was a popular resort of the neighborhood, where, almost every evening, a certain hero of those parts who was called Jack the Rat, entertained late audiences by biting off the heads of live rats.

THE SPIRITUAL UNREST.

A CONVERSION IN SING SING PRISON.

Here, in a dilapidated old building, Jerry McAuley and his wife opened, in 1872, the first of the now well-known type of rescue missions. As a boy Jerry never had a chance. Everything was against him. He had grown up in the worst possible environment, where his heroes were thieves and his instructors were drunkards; an environment which still exists in New York for thousands of boys and young men. Naturally he became both a thief and a drunkard, and being of a daring nature he soon attained wide notoriety as a river pirate. Before he was twenty years old he had reached the natural result of such a career and had been sentenced to Sing Sing prison for fifteen years and six months. A rude preacher of that day was "Awful" Gardner, a former prize-fighter and tough whom Jerry had known as a boy. Gardner came to preach to the prisoners at Sing Sing, telling his own story in his own way. It was a rough sort of personal conviction that he had, and he knew the life of the men before him. Jerry was touched, and his conduct and life

THE SLUM MISSION

were immediately changed, so much so that he was pardoned by Governor Dix.

When he left the prison he had no place to go except to his old haunts in the Bowery and no friends to look after him, and not unnaturally he fell victim again to the environment into which he was so heartlessly cast. For months he was a riotous drunkard, worse than he ever had been before. One night he overheard a missionary preacher talking with a woman; he said that he heard only one word, the name of Jesus, and he decided again to reform. He went with the missionary that night and signed a pledge, but the next day he found it no easier to earn a living honestly than he had before—for he had no training and no knowledge of an honest life. Nor did he have a single friend who knew how to make a living except by stealing. After a day or two of trial the Bowery again overwhelmed him and he deliberately abandoned his idea of reforming and set out with a companion on a marauding expedition. By chance the two met the missionary, who said:

"Jerry, where are you going?"

"I can't starve," said Jerry sullenly.

THE SPIRITUAL UNREST

"Jerry," said the missionary, "come with me. I will pawn this coat before I will see you starve."

Jerry looked the coat over and saw that it would not bring fifty cents at the pawn-shop. Then he said:

"If you think enough of me to do that, I'll die before I steal."

THE FIRST RESCUE MISSION.

From that moment he began the hard upward struggle. Five different times he fell and became riotously drunk, but he kept doggedly at it and finally succeeded. Four years later, after he had thoroughly schooled and tested himself, he started his little mission. At first he met every sort of ridicule, opposition and persecution; at one time hot coals were thrown out of a window upon him, but he continued every night to tell his story to the crowds of "bums" and toughs who gathered in his small room. It was the simplest kind of story of individual salvation through faith in God.

Ever since then the meetings have continued, not Sundays only, with a closed church during

THE SLUM MISSION

the remainder of the week, but every day in the year, with the mission open from early morning until late at night. Jerry died years ago, but his work has gone around the world, the idea of the rescue mission having been adopted in scores of cities.

I wish to give as clear an idea as possible of what such work means and to what extent it is effective, or ineffective. To some of those accustomed to the soft surroundings of uptown religion, a mission of the slums is repellent, not less in the character of the people who attend, than in the nature of the religious expression. But there are deep realities here, too, if we are willing to look for them.

Walk into the small, narrow, stuffy hall of the McAuley Mission any night of the year and you will find the seats filled with the last and lowest dregs of humanity—men who are thieves, ex-convicts and drunkards. Every sort of humanity indeed, from the university man downward, may here be found; they have all reached the last equality of degradation. Around on the walls you will see lettered some of the most striking promises from the New Testament. In front, on the platform, sit a

THE SPIRITUAL UNREST.

number of men and a few women, with the leading musician at the piano. The air is not fresh, not at all fresh; it could not be with such an audience of rags and dirt and drunkenness. Nor are the sights and sounds pleasant to fastidious senses. But wait, we are at the very bottom of the ladder, and there are significant things here too, things well for all of us to know.

WHERE DRUNKARDS COME.

What do all these men come here for? Well, they come for various reasons, comparatively few directly for religious purposes. It is a cold night and they have no place to sleep, so they come in, homeless and drunken, for a chance to rest for a little while, where it is warm. Once a week they are fed liberally, and every night a few of them receive tickets entitling them to a lodging-house bed. Sordid business it seems, doesn't it? A common criticism is that these missions are a mere encouragement to vagrancy.

But are the motives which draw many of the people into the rich uptown churches so fundamentally different? I wonder, is it

THE SLUM MISSION

better to go to church to seek social connections, or business relationships, or to exhibit a new bonnet, than it is to go to church for a corned-beef sandwich?

Anyway, for whatever purpose, these poor and ragged men are here, and no one can tell what is going on in the souls under these rags, any more than one can tell what is going on underneath the gorgeous raiment at St. Bartholomew's Church. If all the worldly were turned into the streets, I wonder, would the Fifth Avenue temple fare better or worse than the slum mission?

Many curious and significant differences exist between the methods of the McAuley Mission and those of the prouder churches. Here no one preaches to anyone else. No one argues any dogmas or creeds; there is almost no sort of ceremony practiced.

Down here people have learned deep things out of life itself. They have been shaken down and tried out. What they want is not books or doctrines or advice or churches; all these superficial things they have spent out with their money and got beyond. Any religion that touches them has got to *live,* and show visible works; there is no other way around it, or about it.

STORIES TOLD AT THE MISSION.

And so the religious service at the McAuley Mission is made up almost exclusively of pages out of the book of common life. It is storytelling—true stories, stories like that of the blind man who said: "One thing I know, that, whereas I was blind, now I see." Is there any more convincing evidence? So they get up in the Mission, men who are cleanly clad, who look clean, and tell what has happened to them, personally. The stories are much alike, for the human experiences which lie behind them are much alike. There is always the bed-rock of conscious and utter failure; there is always the real evidence of salvation. "The difference between the audiences down here and those in uptown churches," one of the workers said to me, "is that these men know they are sinners; uptown they don't know it."

Here is a somewhat typical story I heard at the McAuley Mission:

"I came in here two years, six months and

THE SLUM MISSION

ten days ago, a drunken wretch. I was down and out. I had no hope left. I felt here that Jesus Christ had the power to save me when I could not save myself. I surrendered to him. Since then my life has been changed. I am no longer a slave of drink. I have a job and a good living. I have become reconciled with my family, and I stand here to-night to show what religion can do for a man."

It is impossible to give a true conception of these stories, because a mere report of what is said cannot convey the earnestness and simplicity with which the words are spoken.

Carping criticism may say what it will about such a story, but it cannot touch that man. He knows what he has got, and those wretches who hear him—do they not understand intimately what he has suffered? And do they not also long blindly for the power he has won for himself?

Every one connected with the Mission, from the superintendent, John H. Wyburn, down, has had the same sort of experience; he is on a common plane of life with the men who crowd the little room; he can touch them directly and intimately. He can give them life. One night, when I was there, I heard a Bowery man named Chris, tell his story. Like Jerry McAuley, he had grown up on the Bowery, a street waif. In a city of boasted schools he had grown up without knowing how to read or write. "When they put me in at one door of the school," he said, "I ran out at the other." He was a thief and a drunkard; he had often been arrested; but finally he had stumbled by chance into the mission to get something to eat. There his life was changed. His story, told with the Bowery twang, and dealing with places in the Bowery familiar to all, and relating the particulars of his own resurrection from death, was tremendously impressive. He has now learned to read, and he has a good position where he makes an honest living for the first time in his life. As he told his story he reiterated again and again:

"This is a reality. This is true."

Every night many men come "forward for prayers"—which heaven knows they need—but most of them are impostors, known to be impostors, who come merely on the chance of getting a bed-ticket, or a dime, or a sandwich—and yet from among these abject men,

THE SLUM MISSION

some are reached and lifted. Nothing impressed me more than the infinite patience exercised with these men. The leaders watch for the veriest spark of the new life that they may fan it into flame.

"You have to exercise great patience," I said to Mr. Wyburn.

"Yes," he replied, "someone exercised great patience with me twenty years ago when I came in here a hopeless drunkard—or I should not be here to-night."

They never give up, these leaders, nor do they reject any man, no matter how hopeless he may seem; for have they not had miracles in their own lives? They act on the motto:

MOST WRETCHED—MOST WELCOME.

"The most welcome are those who are the most wretched."

S. H. Hadley, one of the former leaders of the Mission, himself a reconstructed drunkard, once said:

"We love the drunkard because he is a drunkard, and because nobody else does love him. . . . He is asked no questions, no promises are exacted, he has no rules to observe except the one rule of order. He is not lectured on his past, he is not exhorted to lead a better life in the future. He is loved, treated kindly, and joins in prayers night and morning and attends the meetings. Although it is essentially a religious institution, religion is not forced upon him; he is neither watched nor suspected. He is treated as a brother. He is puzzled and don't know what to make of it. Sometimes he comes to the conclusion he has a 'graft' and proceeds to work it for all it is worth. He steals whatever he can lay his hands on and clears out. Sooner or later he is driven back again by hunger, as the only place where he can find food or shelter. On his return he is met with the same welcome, the same kindness. There is no word of reproof or scolding. Again and again he may show the cloven foot, but in the end he finds that in the missions founded by Jerry McAuley there is a stock of love and patience not to be exhausted. That here, if not elsewhere, the spirit of the founder of Christianity lives and moves and endures."

And the leaders and workers of the Mc-

THE SLUM MISSION

Auley Mission, like the Catholic priests, are always at their work. Mr. Wyburn lives with his family in the rooms over the Mission, and he makes a home and a rallying place both for the men who, having been converted, volunteer night after night to help with the work, and for the struggling new converts. I took dinner with the group one evening; it included some half dozen men with their wives and children. Every man there, and some of them are now prosperous business men in New York City, had gone through the fire of just such experiences as I have described. Many of them, in gratitude, devote practically all the spare time of their lives in helping the Mission work, not only giving what money they can, but giving themselves in personal service night after night.

"If you'd been saved from what I have," said one of the men, "you'd be willing to give something in return."

THE FRIENDLIEST PLACE IN NEW YORK.

Another man told me of his well-to-do earlier life, of his ambitions and of his final

THE SPIRITUAL UNREST

downfall. When he finished his story he paused, and then added, looking around the small, plainly furnished room:

"This is the friendliest place in New York."

One night I attended an anniversary. When a convert has stood fast for a year, he has an anniversary. For the first time he leads the meeting, and he tells his story at length for the first time. I attended the anniversary of a young Scotchman named Andy. He had been brought up in a good Scotch home, had become a drunkard and gambler, had been cast off, had drifted much about the world and had finally been cast up among the other human wreckage upon the Bowery. A year ago he had come into the Mission drunk. His life was changed; he had been taken into the little circle upstairs, he had helped as a cook—for these men are willing to do anything in getting hold again—and now, after a year, he told with husky voice of his experience, including the news that he had been reconciled with his family in Scotland, and hoped to go home again soon. And there was real rejoicing over the good fortune of this rehabilitated man.

THE SLUM MISSION

I wish, indeed, I had space here to narrate more of these stories of struggle, reconstruction and human helpfulness, and to tell more of the men I met, but I cannot here find the space. Nor can I speak of the splendid activities of other missions and churches which are struggling with the problems of the poor and the outcast; the work of such men as Elsing of the De Witt Memorial Church, Bates of the Spring Street Church, Cocks of the Church of the Sea and Land, Dowkontt of the Mariner's Temple, and others. Whenever I went downtown to see this work I always came away hopeful, impressed with the feeling that I had touched something that was real; an inspiration that I seldom felt when I went to the great churches uptown.

The point I wish to make most emphatically is that here in this Mission of the slums, among the lowest of the low, is demonstrated again and again the power of a living religion to reconstruct the individual human life. And it apparently makes not the slightest difference whether the man is an unlettered Chris or a university graduate, the power of reconstruction is the same. Once grasped, such religious faith changes the whole world for the man who grasps it. It cures, as it did in apostolic times, both bodies and souls, and it produces, moreover, a singularly simple and brotherly relationship among those who are reached, a desire to serve one another. It is no affectation which causes these men to refer to one another as "Brother." They *are* brothers.

I have endeavored thus to give a picture of one of the best types I know of that sort of religious work which emphasizes the salvation of individual souls. And yet one cannot with open-mindedness study the McAuley Mission and others like it which are doing an honest work, without coming away full of the gravest doubts and questionings. All of the surroundings of the honest mission (how much more detestable the travesties of the occasional fraudulent Mission!), all of the misery, the degradation, the abject hypocrisy, are intensely repellent to the ordinary man or woman. By turns they arouse one's scorn and wring one's deepest sensibilities. They cry out for one's compassion. And even though it is apparent that a man here and there is lifted out of the morass, one comes away from such a mission

THE SLUM MISSION

filled with a conviction as deep as his soul that in some way the whole spectacle of horror and misery is grotesquely and irretrievably wrong. Why should there be any Bowery?

For how can such things be in an age which calls itself civilized? Why should not a civilized nation provide a better school of training than the Bowery for bold and original boys like Jerry McAuley? Why, indeed, should there be any Bowery? Why should the saloon keeper be more friendly than the church? Why all these potent agencies for tearing down and ruining men and women, and why, after having ruined tens of thousands of souls, should a few feeble missions be maintained to drag away, here and there, a single man from out of the wholesale wreckage?

Over and over again the men saved at the missions have the same experience that Jerry McAuley had. A man is converted and then goes back into the hell of his old environment. In the Bowery his old companions await him, every visible thing conspires against him, and nine chances in ten he falls again. A few, a very few will, indeed, win their way into the new atmosphere and the friendly influence of the little upper rooms like those of Mr. Wyburn at the McAuley Mission, but the most will go out again to mean and dirty homes and lodging houses, and a heart-rending search for work, with the ever-enticing and friendly saloon always ready to appease their despondency. If one of them by remote chance should seek the new environment of an uptown church, what do you suppose would happen to him?

I made inquiries among many missions as to the proportion of men and women coming to the missions who were permanently converted. Of those only who "come forward and ask for prayers"—a small proportion, of course, of those who attend—from one to ten per cent., according to the estimates of various experienced workers, are "saved" or converted permanently. Five per cent. would probably be a liberal estimate. In other words, for every five men rehabilitated among those who "inquire," ninety-five go on downward into a very real hell of degradation. While religion is feebly getting at five men, our civilization is hopelessly ruining not only the ninety-five others who "inquire" but the hundreds

THE SLUM MISSION

upon hundreds who come to the missions and do not "go forward," to say nothing of the thousands upon thousands of miserable creatures who never visit the missions at all! How futile the church seems under such circumstances! Is it any wonder that the clergy should be discouraged? Is it any wonder that the people should be crowding the church aside and looking to new ways of producing better results in our civilization?

More than this—far more than this—consider even the five per cent. saved by the Mission. A man cannot be a drunkard or a thief, nor a woman a prostitute for one, or five, or twenty years, and come out in most cases, although converted, and be the same, strong, sure, serviceable man or woman he or she would have been without passing through such horrors. These men are "saved"; that is, they have made peace for themselves, personally, for a few years, but as a general rule they have become more or less ineffective as human instruments. And oftentimes their health is so far ruined that they do not survive many years. Society has helped to ruin them; society must bear the loss.

IS REVIVALISM SUCCESSFUL?

Much the same generalization applies to every great revival of religion. Mighty enthusiasm is stirred up. Men are brought to a realization of God, they acquire a new faith, they feel kindly toward all people—but when they go out into the world again, and try to practice that brotherhood of men which is the only visible proof of the love of God, and to live by the Golden Rule, they find themselves in that Bowery which is the business world, or that jungle which is political life—where the laws that prevail are the laws of the jungle—strife, envy, covetousness—everything to promote hatred, little to promote love. Is it any wonder that most of the converted soon become "backsliders"? The conditions of the world suffocate the religious spirit.

This brings me to the second type of religious work which I wish to present in this chapter—the type which has come to the conclusion that an effort must be made to reach and cure the *causes* of degradation, as well as to save a few of the victims. In this new vision of usefulness the priest is only following the doctor. For years, typhoid fever, for example, meant wholesale death except for a few individuals plucked out of danger by costly and drastic measures. Now the doctor, having investigated causes, demands that the water miles away in the hills be filtered, and the wells of the distant milkman be cleansed. The doctor has learned that most physical diseases are due to social neglect and while still prepared to treat desperate cases with amputation or drastic medicines, the main work of the medical profession lies now in the realm of prevention and hygiene. It is social work.

But the church learns more slowly! It is so cumbered with traditions, so worldly, so divided within itself, so fearful that by means of some new truth which God gives to men He will somehow abolish Himself! The priest often lacks the faith of the doctor! He may see that the spreading disease of unbrotherliness has its origin, in large measure, in the injustice of modern industrial and business conditions, which grind down the poor and the weak, the children, the women, the foreigner—but how falteringly he strikes at these causes, how he palliates with excuses, how he avoids the direct issue! Often, he not only fails to demand changed conditions, but he becomes the chief apologist for the maintenance of the present evil environment!

But churches here and there have begun, seriously, the task of changing social environment. I shall describe the Christ Presbyterian Church as one of the best examples I know of this new sort of religious activity.

A NEW SORT OF RELIGIOUS ACTIVITY.

Christ Church is affiliated with and supported largely by the Brick Presbyterian Church, one of the most notable of the rich churches of the Fifth Avenue district. It is on the West Side of New York City, in Thirty-sixth Street, near Eighth Avenue, in a neighborhood occupied exclusively by wage-earners, clerks and small shopkeepers, largely German by extraction, with, recently, a rapid incrowding of a poorer population of Italians and Negroes. Christ Church, like so many other small churches in New York, had its beginnings in a Sunday School. One Sunday afternoon, more than fifty years ago, a group of earnest young men, one of whom, John E.

THE SLUM MISSION

Parsons, a distinguished lawyer and a director of the Sugar Trust, is still living, went down among the working people and gathered in a group of boys from off the streets. The school grew. Mr. Parsons was for years its superintendent—a position more recently held by his son, Herbert Parsons, now congressman and political leader in New York state. A church was finally organized and a large building of the old type was constructed. By the old type I mean a Sunday Church, open one day in the week for religious services, and closed for the most part during the remaining days of the week.

But for the times it was considered a reasonably good work; hundreds of churches in New York City to-day (and elsewhere) are still slumberously conducting Sunday churches and are apparently at ease in Zion. Indeed, there was more interest in this Mission than in most, for a few volunteer laymen, men like Mr. Parsons, William D. Barbour and others, took a keen interest, especially in the Sunday School. Money was contributed liberally and preaching was steadily maintained.

And yet, at no time in its history did the

church have more than four hundred and fifty members, out of an immediate neighborhood with a population of from 15,000 to 20,000 people. As a vital or commanding influence upon the common daily lives of these swarming thousands it was, of course, hardly more than negligible. How could it be otherwise? Even the earnest volunteer workers who came down from Fifth Avenue once a week knew and could know next to nothing at all about the buyings and sellings, the births and the marryings and the buryings, the hopes and fears and joys which make up the great part of the lives of these working people. They lived in a wholly foreign sphere. Two or three admirable paid workers were on the ground all the time, but among the crowding thousands of the population of the neighborhood a few women and a busy pastor count for comparatively little.

I am saying these things not in criticism of Christ Church; I am merely pointing out conditions more or less common to all New York church work—conditions of which the clergy themselves have been the sharpest critics.

Out of the conviction that the old Christ

THE SLUM MISSION

Church was not the power in the community that it should be, that, indeed, it was losing its hold on the common lives of men, grew the new Christ Church—a seven-day church—the work of which I wish here to consider. No essentially new ideas were adopted by the Brick Church in the reconstruction of this branch of its work. It was the result of a widespread spiritual unrest, both inside and outside of the churches, which was expressed here in a social settlement, there in more scientific charity organizations, and in many other social and civic activities. It was a part of the present ethical revival. Dr. Rainsford and Dr. Judson had shown the way toward the institutional church, and they in their turn had learned much from the social settlements.

The new Christ Church, then, is an institutional church. That is, besides its places for Sunday worship and Bible schools, fully half of its building is devoted to various social and neighborhood purposes, with rooms for clubs, classes and amusements. And it is open seven days in the week. In short, it is an effort to reach and serve more of the people of the neighborhood, to touch them on more sides of

THE SPIRITUAL UNREST

their lives, and to influence them more continuously.

Three men of vision inspired and made possible the construction of the new church—three successive pastors of the Brick Church. Dr. Henry Van Dyke began the work; it was continued through the brief pastorate of Maltbie D. Babcock, and it was completed by the late minister, W. R. Richards.

Many of the older church missions were poor and cheap affairs, built on the principle that almost anything was good enough for the poor, but in many respects Christ Church is a better, more beautiful, and more commodious building than the mother church. When Dr. Richards first went to see it after it was completed, he said:

"The best thing about this place is that it is better than anything we have got ourselves."

The building has been open now for four years, an able leader, the Rev. James M. Farr, has been in charge of it, and while its activities have not been as extensive or as costly as those of St. George's or St. Bartholomew's, they have been developed and maintained with enlightened energy.

THE SLUM MISSION

WHAT AN INSTITUTIONAL CHURCH DOES

I think no one could visit either the church house on a week day, or see the Sunday School on Sunday with eight hundred children in attendance, without being greatly impressed. There is life here! The church is open all day long—open longer than the public schools, and more days in the week—but not open as long as the saloons and nickel theaters, cigar stores and candy parlors, which are to be found in numbers everywhere. A schedule of activities in the entrance-hall gives one an impressive idea of how the days are filled, and of the variety and extent of the work attempted. Two large kindergartens are held in the morning for some ninety little children. Older children and young people are organized in clubs and classes which meet at various hours during the week. Instruction is given in carpentry, sewing, cooking, typewriting and basketry. A boy's cadet corps is drilled regularly. To provide for the amusement which human nature will have (in the saloon, if not in the church) there are billiard tables, a bowling alley, a shooting gallery, a gym-

THE SPIRITUAL UNREST

nasium and baths, and a room for games. In the summer, excursions to the country are constantly being organized. A considerable library is provided and the books are widely used in the neighborhood. The McAlpin literary society and the Glee Club give plays and other entertainments, including social dances.

A catalogue of activities such as this seems dry enough and it cannot, of course, convey the cheerful spirit of association and helpfulness that pervades the work. The church provides an outlet into the finer and pleasanter things of life for an over-worked people whose low wages and poor homes give them few opportunities. It gets them together, it lets them see something of the people from uptown, and better than that, it lets the people from uptown see something of them; it tends to awaken that sympathy between man and man which is the fundamental note of democracy.

Dr. Farr says that one of the chief purposes of the work is simply to make people happy; to give them a greater interest in life.

"Happiness makes for religion," he says,

THE SLUM MISSION

"quite as much as religion makes for happiness."

Youthful activities, which once spent themselves in destructive and lawless amusements now have, in such institutions, an organized outlet—organized clubs, organized classes, organized sports, organized gymnastics. Since the settlements and institutional churches have appeared in the large cities the old gangs of hoodlums, which formerly menaced the poorer parts of the city, have almost wholly disappeared. Such work prevents at least some of the conditions which produced Jerry McAuley.

Illness among the poor is one of the influences which tend to produce hopelessness and deterioration; an institutional church can, therefore, do much toward making the environment of life easier by ministering to the sick. Christ Church maintains a clinic with a physician on hand at stated times, and a visiting nurse is constantly employed.

A tuberculosis class similar to those which I describe in a coming chapter is also maintained with success. Some of the patients find a place to rest out-of-doors on the roof of the church. I saw a group of them there, wrapped in rugs, sitting in steamer chairs and looking most comfortable.

While statistics do not convey an idea of the spirit which animates this work, it is interesting to know that a staff of 17 salaried workers, five men and twelve women, are employed to do the work, and there are, besides, about 175 volunteer workers, mostly in the Sunday School, who give occasional service.

Here, then, is an effort to reach and improve the social life of the neighborhood which is, of course, lacking in institutions such as the McAuley Mission. So far as it goes, and up to the extent of its capacity, it is undoubtedly a great influence in its community; it tends to leaven the hard lump of unfriendliness and to give a vital meaning to religion.

Not for a moment would I say anything that would hinder or injure such progressive work in any way; and yet, if we are to understand the problem which to-day confronts the church in New York, we must inquire how far the institutional church has now reached in its tremendous task of changing the environment of the people of the poorer neighborhoods.

THE SLUM MISSION

IS THE INSTITUTIONAL CHURCH A SUCCESS?

On the strictly ecclesiastical side—that is, if we measure by statistics—Christ Church has shown little progress in four years. Its membership has increased only from about 500 to 536, while its Sunday School, with an enrollment of 1,000 pupils, always an enthusiastic work, has with difficulty been maintained at its full strength. On the other hand, the social activities have reached an increasing number of people, and have helped in some degree to feed the religious services and the Sunday School. Over 500 people make use of the building every day in the week, and there are 2,500 names on the roll, representing 1,000 families. And yet, compared with the swarming population of the neighborhood, this number is small indeed. A single nickel theater around the corner attracts two or three times as many people every day as all the free attractions of Christ Church put together—and as for the saloons, they have not lost their popularity! The people reached are nearly all of American or German stock; practically none of the thousands of Italians and Negroes of the neighborhood are touched in any way.

I am not giving these facts in any spirit of criticism, or arguing that Christ Church could or should do more than it is doing. I am merely trying to give an idea of the immensity of the problem, and the strength of the opposing forces.

The church is, indeed, trying to touch life in new ways, but as yet even the institutional activities touch only a little fringe of it, inspire or amuse or train, only a very few of the swarming population. The church scarcely touches, as yet, the vital problems of everyday life of the neighborhood—the buying and selling, the work, the play, the deepest hopes and fears and joys of the people. And these are the things which tear down or build up the life of individual men and women.

Moreover, the work of the church is largely with children; a work, indeed, necessary to be done, and of the highest value. But upon coming of age most of the young people drift away; and rarely return to the influence of the religious activities. Neither Christ Church nor any other gets and holds many men, es-

THE SLUM MISSION

pecially in the poorer parts of town. Though the institutional churches do make a few lives happier and more hopeful, the great mass of the people must still live in the most sordid surroundings; they must work long hours at low wages, and the slightest accident precipitates them below the poverty line. Life is a daily struggle for bare maintenance not only for the men but for many of the women and children. Under such circumstances is it any wonder that the play of the clubs and classes at the church, not to speak of the religious services, seem distant and unreal? Why should they bother with them? It is all right for the children, but does it help to meet the tremendous grown-up problems of employment, or the incalculable worries and alarms of unemployment, of paying rent, of buying food and clothing? What has the church to offer in the way of changing such familiar conditions as those presented in the following sober report of the Tenement House Commission of New York?

"The tenement districts of New York are places in which thousands of people are living in the smallest space in which it is possible for human beings to exist—crowded together in dark, ill-ventilated rooms in many of which the sunlight never enters, and in most of which fresh air is unknown. They are centers of disease, poverty, vice and crime, where it is a marvel not that some children grow up to be thieves, drunkards and prostitutes, but that so many should ever grow up to be decent and self-respecting. All the conditions which surround childhood, youth and womanhood in New York's crowded tenement quarters make for unrighteousness. They also make for disease. There is hardly a tenement house in which there has not been at least one case of pulmonary tuberculosis within the last five years, and in some houses there have been as great a number as twenty-two different cases of this terrible disease.

"The most terrible of all the features of tenement house life in New York, however, is the indiscriminate herding of all kinds of people in close contact; the fact, that, mingled with the drunken, the dissolute, the improvident, the diseased, dwell the great mass of the respectable workingmen of the city with their families."

THE SLUM MISSION

A CHURCH DEALING WITH CHILDREN.

The plain fact is, the church, even the institutional church, is still content with a religion that is a thing apart, that concerns only small, superficial things, that deals with children. Can any religion really live that does not apply itself frankly to every side of human life—business, industry, banking, tenement houses, landowning, in short, the *whole* of life? Or can the church recover from its present decadent condition until it strikes to the very roots of social conditions?

In one small but significant department of its work Christ Church actually strikes down into a real problem of the tenements: coal. It has a message of helpfulness about coal. Coal is ordinarily sold to poor families by the basket and the profits to the dealers are extortionate; it is one way of bleeding the poor. So Christ Church has a coal club of about one hundred women who pay in ten cents or more a week. The club buys its coal in quantities and each member is assigned her particular share, thus eliminating the extortionate small dealer. The club is wholly self-supporting—a thoroughly democratic institution. A little common good, a little brotherliness has here crept into the coal business of the West Side. I wonder what would be the result of more such coöperation, let us say in the making of clothing, the buying of groceries, the ownership of tenements?

The rich people of the uptown churches, indeed, have the poor on their consciences as never before. To meet the condition they have built institutional churches—a good idea, so far as it goes. They are willing to pay a large proportion of the expenses of maintenance, or even all of the expenses; they are willing that the institutional churches should be finer than their own churches; they will even go down and help with the clubs, classes and Sunday Schools. In all these superficial things, in the singing and praying, they are willing to coöperate; but that is as far as they have got at present. There the coöperation stops short!

When it comes to extending their religion to a coöperation in business and politics, to banking and landowning—why, no, *that* cannot be. For "business is business"—and re-

THE SLUM MISSION

ligion must be kept out of it. They have a groping idea that the church, if it is to survive, must command the lives of workingmen (how much we have heard of "The Church and the Working Man," "The Church and the Foreigner," and so on), but they are not themselves willing to let religion command their own lives. They worship with the workingman and then turn around and charge him an exorbitant rental for the home he lives in, they take fat profits on the necessaries of life, they work women and little children long hours at low wages—and out of the proceeds they live luxuriously, while the workingman scrapes along miserably in his tenements. No, it is not *real*—this religion. It is "Brother" only on Sunday, and the masses of grown men and women in poor neighborhoods know it. They prefer the honest openness of the saloon, the frank cheapness of the nickel theater, where they can pay for what they get, to the doubtful largess of the church.

IN THE RICH CHURCHES.

And at the same time that the church among the tenements perishes for want of a message upon the vital problems of life, so it perishes uptown from a different sort of superficiality. It no more reaches the real life of the rich than it reaches the real life of the poor. For example, on Easter Sunday I visited four of the richest churches in the Fifth Avenue district. I never saw before such a gorgeous crowd, such evidences of wealth, so many automobiles, so much expensive dressing— such elaborate displays of flowers, such costly music.

It was, indeed, a great and splendid show— a show both outside and inside the church— a time when, for once, it was fashionable to go to church.

"Easter," said the New York *Times* on that Sunday morning, "promises to be celebrated with unusual impressiveness throughout this city to-day. . . . Never, according to the florists and milliners have there been more extensive preparations. . . . Forty per cent. more flowers have been sold this year than were sold last season.

"The women will wear foulards and cashmeres in mauve, mahogany and brown, the gowns will be cut in the Moyen age style, the line of the gown not being at the waist line, but eight inches below—about half-way between the waist and the knees. Peach basket hats will be discarded for the new Paris style."

And for the men, too, it was a great celebration.

"Waistcoats," continues the *Times*, "will be of *khaki* tan, or even of a plain sky blue. Ascot ties will be worn with high hats. The ties will be a shade darker than the waistcoats, and flowered."

> " I went into the church to find my Lord.
>   They said, He is here:
>   He lives here.
>   But I could not see Him
>   For the creed-tablets and bonnet-flowers."

So the church wanes and sickens in New York. A few earnest churches and missions drag men here and there from the gutter, but the gutter itself, the gutter of unbrotherliness, of the oppression of the weak and the luxury of the strong, still engulfs its thousands and carries them down to ruin. Much of the reconstructive power and vision is outside the churches, not inside; it is found in settlements, charity and civic organizations and among socialists.

I asked a man who has gained wisdom where people are poor, why men are not attracted to the church.

"Because," he said, "we never ask them to do anything heroic, or anything really well worth doing. We demand no sacrifices from them. What can a man to-day *do* in the church? About the only thing he can do is to pass the collection plate and count the pennies afterwards—that is, he can do the trifling business of the church. Even when he gives money he rarely makes a genuine sacrifice."

It is only when the poor devils downtown in the McAuley Mission "surrender," and admit religion to the whole of their lives, that they are reconstructed, and the rich devils uptown can achieve reconstruction in no other way. Nor can the church be saved by giving a little money for missions, nor by going down to the workingman on Sunday; it must be all or nothing.

CHAPTER V

HEALING THE SICK IN THE CHURCHES

AN ACCOUNT OF THE EMMANUEL MOVEMENT.

MANY Protestant churches in various parts of the country—not to speak of hundreds of Christian Science churches—are now conducting "religious clinics" or health services for the healing of the sick. Beginning with the work of the Reverend Dr. Elwood Worcester and his associate, the Reverend Dr. Samuel McComb, at Emmanuel Church in Boston in 1906, the movement has spread with a rapidity which indicates that it must have met a genuine human need.

On the other hand, many doctors, health departments and hospitals are extending their work into wholly new fields, social, psychic, philanthropic, which were formerly more or less within the province of the church. Both minister and physician, in these times of spiritual unrest, have grown discontented with their former successes. A new relationship is seen to exist between religion and medicine. Religion is reaching out over debatable ground to do the work of the doctor; the doctor is reaching out over debatable ground to do the work of the church.

What, then, are these extraordinary new movements? How did they originate, what are they doing now, what are their possibilities and limitations? In answering these questions we shall not only come to a more complete understanding of the new movements but we shall be able to see something of the conditions of spiritual unrest to which they are evident responses.

For years past Emmanuel Church has been regarded as one of the most successful churches in Boston. It has had the largest membership of any Episcopal church in the city. It has had a wealthy and generous following. It has had able ministers. No other church in Boston and few in America have gone further with institutional activities, for none has felt more keenly the need of some agency to soften the strain of modern eco-

HEALING THE SICK

nomic relationships. Its clubs, classes, camps, gymnasiums, its hospital work and other activities are widespread and highly developed. In Emmanuel Memorial house, located in one of the poorer neighborhoods of Boston, is conducted what is to all intents and purposes a social settlement. An examination of the year book of the church is a revelation of extraordinary activities such as no church of twenty years ago would have dreamed of undertaking.

A DISCONTENTED CHURCH.

And yet, somehow, all this success, these widespread activities were not enough. Something was lacking. Dr. Elwood Worcester, the rector, wrote in one of his annual reports:

"The people are very willing to accept what we offer them in the way of fine parish buildings, libraries, gymnasiums, music, trade-schools, art classes, and, in some instances, baths; and these things are of incalculable importance as elements of a well-ordered life. But the best that the Christian church has to offer men is the religion of Jesus Christ, and this all our social endeavors do not seem to make our people particularly anxious to receive at our hands."

Dr. Worcester also voices the disheartenment of the ministry over the fact that the churches are not performing their function.

"I have heard many of the ablest and most conscientious clergymen of our church confess with tears that they are doing this (social) work with a sense of despondency and humiliation because they do not feel that they are giving their people the best they have to give. In other words, the Church of Christ cannot maintain and propagate itself by anything less comprehensive, less spiritual and tremendous than the Christian religion, and the plain truth is, we are not bringing the full force of our religion to bear upon the hearts and lives of the people."

It was this deep conviction of failure that caused Dr. Worcester and Dr. McComb to try the experiment which has resulted in the truly notable Emmanuel Movement. They asked themselves what it was, in times past, that made the church strong. Was it not the fact that the church had something to give to men

HEALING THE SICK

and women which, down in their hearts, they desired above everything else? In its periods of real power and faith, the church has never been compelled to seek men; at such times men have passionately sought the church.

"The Christian religion began its mission," says Dr. Worcester, "with an enormous sense of power. Taking its stand in the very center of the universe—the soul of man—the church had gifts to bestow, gifts for all. In those days no one touched the religion without being transformed by it."

HOW THE CHURCH HAS LOST ITS HOLD.

The problem was how to re-inspire the church with its old faith and power. The failure in the past has been due to no lack of willingness on the part of the ministry. Thousands of leaders of the church would willingly lay down their lives if they might experience the joy of transforming men's lives. Nothing, indeed, is more pathetic in this world than the spectacle of the good man who is seeking to do good, but cannot. Instead of increasing power in the church, the ministry has seen its influence lessening. Uncounted Americans whose ancestors looked to the church as the chief inspiration of their daily existence no longer attend any church. Other thousands, though still nominally members or attendants, have ceased to admit the church or its ministers as a really vital influence in their lives. With expensive equipment, large funds, an educated clergy, often costly music and other attractions, the church, taken as a whole, no longer leads or even deeply stirs the American people. Able young men do not go into the ministry as they once did; last year there were seven hundred fewer students in fifty-eight Protestant theological seminaries than there were twelve years ago. Ministers generally are underpaid and often disheartened with the prevailing apathy and neglect. Many churches, especially in the east, stand empty and deserted.

The Catholic church has apparently fared better than the Protestant churches, because it has been constantly recruited from the ever-swelling streams of immigration from the Catholic countries of Southern Europe. But the Catholic church is also discontented. The second generation of foreigners, whether Catholic or Jew, tends to slip away from church influences. A Catholic priest recently put it thus vigorously:

"Americanizing means the loss of the man to the church."

Is not this an extraordinary statement? Is Americanism irreligious?

NEW WAVE OF RELIGIOUS ENTHUSIASM.

But in spite of these striking facts, we hear a clear-sighted observer like Professor James saying that "a wave of religious activity analogous in some respects to the spread of early Christianity, Buddhism and Mohammedanism is passing over our American world." In short, there is not less of moral enthusiasm or spiritual activity in America, rather far more of it, but the church somehow has ceased to lead or inspire it as it did in former times.

Dr. Worcester felt deeply this condition. What should be done, in Emmanuel Church, to get back the power of inspiring and transforming men's lives?

In order to reach any clear understanding of the Emmanuel Movement, it will be necessary to consider, as a foundation, some of the larger movements of modern thought.

The world is just now being swept with a great wave of idealistic philosophy. It is a rebound from the years of materialism and materialistic philosophy which swayed the intellectual and spiritual life of men during a large part of the last century. It is the return of the pendulum of human thought which ever oscillates between the material and the spiritual interpretations of life, less of Herbert Spencer, Huxley and Haeckel, and more of the German idealists and the modern psychologists.

THE NEW IDEALISM.

The new idealism lays its emphasis upon the power of mind over matter, the supremacy of spirit. Its thinkers have interested themselves as never before in the marvelous phenomena of human personality, most of which were contemptuously regarded by the old materialistic science. The wonders of the human mind, the attribute we call consciousness, the self, the relation of mind to mind, telepathy, the strange phenomena of double or

HEALING THE SICK

multiple consciousness, hypnotism, and all the related marvels, are now crowding for serious attention and promise to open to us new worlds of human knowledge.

Now, every great philosophical and scientific movement has its popular and practical reflex. Just as the spread of the materialistic philosophy in the last century was accompanied the world over by a wave of infidelity and agnosticism, among the people, so the present wave of idealistic philosophy finds expression in a number of most remarkable popular movements. Every philosophy has its correlated faith; the faiths of the materialistic nineteenth century were pessimistic, negative, deterministic, while the new faiths are optimistic and positive. "I do not" and "I cannot" are superseded by "I do," "I know," "I will." They are expressed in the spreading and significant Christian Science and New Thought movements, in the rise to power of leaders of the type of Dowie, in the revival of interest in spiritualism as a religion, in the idealistic side of socialism. At the very time that the philosophers and psychologists were *thinking* their way to the new philosophy, P. P. Quimby and Henry Wood and Mrs. Eddy and Dowie and many others were *feeling* their way toward new popular faiths. The world was weary of the old materialism, and the revolt, which some men reasoned out while others only felt, came alike to all.

And necessarily it has deeply affected both religion and medicine. The scientific spirit of the last century, turning its cold, necessary gaze upon the Bible, upon church history, upon religious phenomena, relentlessly cutting away accumulations of superstition and error, for a time dampened and confused the ardor of a primitive faith. Critical examination, coming at a time when the world was also undergoing swift material changes, in which men's minds were consumed with the thirst for wealth and conquest, tended to rob the church of its ancient influence. The churches themselves grew rich and materialistic, and like any other entrenched institution, they have accepted the new idealism with intense reluctance. They are naturally aristocratic and conservative, rather than democratic and liberal. Most of them yield only

HEALING THE SICK

when some diet of defiance is nailed to their doors.

From time to time, indeed, the spirit blazed up in widespread revivals, which were often unconnected with organized religious bodies. It appeared in such democratic revolts as the Salvation Army. It has expressed itself on the ethical side in extraordinary reform movements in politics and industry, but for the most part the church remained unaffected. Divided into warring sects, it busied itself with acrimonious and wearisome disputes over creeds and interpretations; it cast out heretics. It had no sure sense for that which was extinct.

POWER OF CHRISTIAN SCIENCE.

When men and women wanted the spirit of the new idealism they sought it, rightly or wrongly, elsewhere. Men and women flocked to the Christian Science movement; or gave their money and placed their lives in Dowie's hands; or surrendered themselves to the peace of the New Thought; or eagerly, pathetically, sought out the spiritualistic séance; or became passionate socialists, making of socialism a very real religion; or satisfied themselves in an unselfish devotion to reform movements in municipal and state politics—all wholly or mostly outside of the churches. In short, they followed blindly—and are following to-day—any movement which had in it a spark of the new thing their souls required. It is noteworthy that the Christian Scientists have not had to go out for a single convert, nor establish a single costly gymnasium, nor conduct a single settlement; and the socialist, instead of receiving personal advantages for being a member of the party, has willingly paid to join!

Surely there is a deep significance in the fact that hungry people have rushed forward to accept these new faiths, and have been willing to give their lives and their money to sustain them. The new faiths must have something of life and vitality in them—a certain response to the main currents of the world's thought—which cannot be disregarded or overlooked. Tell a Christian Scientist that Mrs. Eddy is a jealous autocrat, or a Dowieite that Dowie was a charlatan, or the revolutionary socialist that his dream of a perfect state is the veriest nonsense, and he will reply, "Whereas I was blind, now I see." Something has changed the man's life, and his conviction, so far as he is concerned, confutes the logic of the wise. It is unanswerable. No church, offering glorious traditions, aristocratic associations, costly music, or clubs or classes, can compete for an instant with a faith which works marvels in men's souls.

Let us now return to the Emmanuel Movement, which may best be approached, perhaps, through the men who originated it.

PERSONALITY OF DR. WORCESTER AND DR. M'COMB.

The Reverend Dr. Elwood Worcester is a stout, solid, vigorous man who wears by preference a business suit and looks like an energetic business man. A lover of outdoor life, no year passes when he does not go hunting in the Rocky Mountains, or fishing in Newfoundland, or exploring and pearl-hunting in Labrador. Born in Ohio, he came up fighting, making his own way. After graduating at Columbia University he told Bishop Potter that he wanted to lay the foundations of his theological training in Germany. But the Bishop objected:

"No," he said; "you stay here and graduate at the seminary; then you will not be tinged with German rationalism."

"If I graduate from the seminary," asked the candidate, "will you then offer any objection to my going to Germany?"

"Not the slightest," said the Bishop.

Fired with his project, Worcester hired a room in a vacant house in New York City, and worked alone all summer long from early morning until late at night. At the opening of the General Seminary in the fall he was able to pass the first two years of the course, and was graduated a year later. True to his promise he returned to the astonished Bishop, who now gave his permission for the candidate to go to Germany. And there, at once, he found himself in the atmosphere of the new thought; he studied under the eminent psychologists Wundt and Fechner and he wrote for his thesis the "Opinions of John Locke." On his return to America he was ordained and after a short experience in church work in Brooklyn, became chaplain and professor of philosophy at Lehigh University.

All along he had been a vigorous and independent thinker. He had accepted broadly the argument of the "higher critics"; his volume, "The Book of Genesis in the Light of Modern Knowledge," in which he voiced the newest thought on the Bible, was published while he was rector of St. Stephen's Church in Philadelphia. He came to Boston in 1904.

Dr. Worcester's co-worker, Dr. Samuel McComb, is an Irishman with the Celtic vividness of mind and personality, a persuasive and magnetic speaker. He was educated at Oxford, and for a time was a minister in the Presbyterian Church. After becoming an Episcopalian he joined Dr. Worcester, and has worked with him upon the closest terms of friendship ever since. Worcester and McComb defended the Reverend Dr. Crapsey when he was tried for heresy.

BEGINNING OF THE EMMANUEL MOVEMENT.

In the fall of 1906 the Emmanuel Movement began. As I have shown, Dr. Worcester was discontented with the work of the church; he felt, as he says, that "the time is come when the church must enter more deeply into the personal lives of the people and make a freer use of the means modern science and the gospel of Christ place at her disposal, if she is to continue even to hold her own."

Acting upon this thought it was most natural that Emmanuel Church should turn to the healing of the physically and mentally sick. It was one of the commands of Christ that his disciples should heal the sick. In certain Catholic churches to-day, Lourdes, the Cathedral of St. Ann de Beauprè, and others, "the lame, the halt and the blind come and are cleansed and go away leaping and singing and praising God." Similar cures have been wrought by Christian Science. Why should the Protestant churches alone have abandoned this important work?

Now, every new religious movement must be based upon two elements: Faith and Reason. If there is Faith alone, unanchored by the very best reason of the times, then the new religion soars away into fanaticism and superstition. If there is Reason alone, then the re-

HEALING THE SICK

ligion, if it can be called religion, sinks into the morass of materialism. As fast as Reason explains a mystery, Faith presents innumerable new mysteries for explanation. As man progresses, old creeds must yield to new; old Faiths, crumbling before advancing Reason, ever give rise to new and greater Faiths.

Dr. Worcester saw the need of the great faith which cures the Catholic who kisses the stone toe of the saint, but he saw also the need of the best reason that science could give for such a cure. A mass of scientific knowledge has been attained by the medical profession; much is known of disease and the cure of disease. Why should all this knowledge be disregarded or discarded? Is not such knowledge also of God?

"Most religious workers," says Dr. Worcester, "in this field (of mental healing) have made the mistake of supposing that God can cure in only one way and that the employment of physical means indicates a lack of faith. This is absurd. God cures by many means. He uses the sunlight, healing and nourishing substances, water and air."

TWO DIFFERENT KINDS OF DISEASES.

Medical science and psychology have shown that a very large proportion of all the diseases from which men suffer—nearly half, in fact —are diseases in which the mind, the personality or the moral nature is the controlling factor—the point at which the vicious circle of physical and psychical misery can be broken. They are called, roughly, functional nervous disorders, and include neurasthenia, hysteria with its myriad forms of simulated organic disease, hypochondria, morbid fears and worries, addiction to alcohol and drugs, and moral disorders of many kinds.

On the other hand, a large group of diseases, called roughly organic disorders, such as smallpox, diphtheria, appendicitis, do not primarily affect the personality.

Formerly the doctor drugged and the surgeon cut impartially for all sorts of diseases. So long as the materialistic interpretation of life was absolutely accepted, medicine tended to become a mere group of scientific formulæ. Given a certain disease its cure was to be

HEALING THE SICK

found on page 269 of the manual. And the whole world was deluged with drugs.

Then Dr. Osler appeared with his declaration that medicine was not a science but an art, in which he showed that there are in reality only a few drugs which are genuine specifics for any disease. But still earlier, the psychologists, beginning with Fechner in 1860, had begun to lay a broad, deep foundation for the study of men's minds and personalities. Wundt (in 1878) established the first psychological laboratory in the world, and in 1883 Professor G. Stanley Hall opened the first laboratory in America. Professor William James published his Psychology and Dr. Pierre Janet began giving to the world his studies in abnormal psychology and the phenomena of multiple consciousness. Many other workers speedily entered the field.

And yet, is it not a marvel that until this year there was not in any medical college in the world any department for the study of the mind? The brain, indeed, is minutely examined; but the mind is disregarded. Is it any wonder, that from a science which regarded men as all body and no mind, no spirit, there should be revolts such as those of Mrs. Eddy and Alexander Dowie? And revolts, especially when inspired with faith, naturally go far—go, indeed, as in Christian Science, to the other extreme, in which men are regarded as all mind and no body. Thus the people, right in their instincts, are forever disciplining the pundits who, with their eyes too closely fixed upon their own theories, become warped and unhuman. At the present time the pundits, not only in medicine but in politics and religion, are being forced to adapt themselves to new lines of thought which they have not hitherto willingly recognized.

FUNDAMENTAL BELIEFS OF EMMANUEL MOVEMENT.

Dr. Worcester and Dr. McComb have attempted to establish no new dogma. They believe profoundly in the power of the mind over the body, that the mind, when inspired, or transformed, can cure many of the diseases of the mind and of the moral nature. It can also help greatly in alleviating pain and producing the state of confidence and hope which

HEALING THE SICK

are favorable to the cure of all other diseases. But organic ailments generally, they believe, must be left to physical treatment, to medicine, surgery, hygiene, isolation and skilled nursing. If a headache is caused by eyestrain, a pair of glasses is far more effective than any mental treatment. If a tooth is bad it must be filled or pulled out. If a leg is crushed it must have the surgeon's knife. A case of yellow fever must be isolated; no amount of mental treatment will prevent the disease from spreading unless it is isolated. In short, the need of the whole man must be met; the doctor and the minister must work together. But before there is an attempt to cure, all the light that science possesses must be thrown upon the disease; there must be a diagnosis. Otherwise, what is to prevent a patient with smallpox or diphtheria wandering into a church full of people and spreading the contagion of his disease?

Two cases at Emmanuel Church show the necessity of a thorough diagnosis. One man came to be treated for neurasthenia; but the history of the case, together with a careful physical examination of the patient, revealed the presence of a cancer in the stomach. Immediate operation was advised and performed, instead of wasting the patient's time by a wholly ineffectual mental treatment. Another case shows the reverse condition. A young man had been treated, drugged and dieted for years for an organic disease of the stomach. Careful examination indicated that the symptoms referable to the stomach were nervous and mental in their origin. Treatment was given to him by Dr. Worcester and he promptly improved.

Thus we find the first meeting of the Emmanuel Movement in 1906 taken part in by Dr. James J. Putnam, one of the foremost neurologists of Boston. It also had the support of such able neurologists and physicians as Dr. Weir Mitchell, Dr. Barker of Johns Hopkins (Dr. Osler's successor), Dr. Richard C. Cabot and many others. Dr. Isador H. Coriat has been associated with the work from the beginning. Professor William James and other psychologists have also been deeply interested in this attempt to apply practically some of the newer teachings and discoveries of psychology.

HEALING THE SICK

THE SUBCONSCIOUS SELF.

It is impossible, in a brief space, to go into anything like a full explanation of the psychological theory upon which the Emmanuel Movement is founded. But in reality it is exceedingly simple. It is based on the belief that underneath the conscious life of every human being resides a subconscious or subliminal self which has powers and energies which only a comparatively few people learn to utilize.

"Men the world over," says Professor James, "possess amounts of resource which only very exceptional individuals push to their extremes of use."

It is supposed that in the phenomenon of hypnotism the conscious personality is put to sleep and that the hypnotist addresses the subconscious personality, so that when the patient awakens, although he will often have no memory of what was said to him while in trance, yet he will follow out the instructions given.

The subconscious mind is also suggestible without hypnosis; that is, it is subject to moral

THE SPIRITUAL UNREST

influence and direction. This is, of course, no new phenomenon. Human beings are constantly suggesting to one another; we practice suggestion every day of our lives. A little girl falls down and hurts herself. Mother kisses the spot and makes it well.

It is possible, then, to exert a profound influence over men's minds by thus asserting or suggesting strength, truth, hope. Many men also learn to exercise the same power over themselves by auto-suggestion. Instead of worry, fear, sin, which cause many of the ills and woes that flesh is heir to, and aggravate many others, the aim is to fill the mind with hope, good thoughts, kindness, courage. And this is no new philosophy, although recently it has been endowed with the power of *faith*.

Long ago, as Professor James says, Spinoza wrote that anything that a man can avoid under the notion that it is bad, he may also avoid under the notion that something else is good. He who habitually acts under the negative notion, the notion of the bad, is called a slave by Spinoza. To him who acts habitually under the notion of good, he gives the name of freeman.

HEALING THE SICK

"I DO" SUPERSEDES "I DO NOT."

The basis of the whole system is a vital belief based partly on religion, partly on the applications of new psychological knowledge that a man is, indeed, largely the master of his fate; that there is new hope for the weakest and the lowest; that if a man will place himself where he is in the current of good and high thoughts, if he says, "I do," "I will," instead of saying weakly and hopelessly, "I cannot," "I do not," his life will become a new thing. This is the phenomenon of the "new birth," the "transformed life." In short, it is a living faith in the free will of men, as against the old fatalism.

Having explained the philosophical foundations upon which the Emmanuel Movement rests, we may now consider the concrete processes of healing, and after that the criticisms which have been leveled against the Movement. Before the hundreds of suffering men and women who came to Emmanuel Church are treated by the ministers they are examined by physicians who are sympathetic with the work, and careful records are kept of every case. Those who require medical treatment only are referred to doctors; those who need mental and religious treatment are sent to Dr. Worcester and Dr. McComb. In reality the treatment is exceedingly simple.

"I place a man in a comfortable reclining chair," says Dr. Worcester, "cut off the stream of external sensation by darkening the room and insuring quiet, and I earnestly tell him that in a few moments he will be asleep. If he knows that hundreds of other persons have undergone this experience he will be more certain to accept my assurance and to obey the suggestion. I visit a woman who has been bedridden for months or years, convince myself that her inability to move does not proceed from true paralysis and I assure her that she can arise and I earnestly command her to do so, which she proceeds to do. A patient with palpitating heart comes to me. I soothe him by a few gentle and quiet words and tell him that his nervousness is passing away, that his heart is beating quietly and regularly and that in a few moments he will be calm and happy. He listens to me, believes me, and the prediction is fulfilled."

HEALING THE SICK

These words of Dr. Worcester concerning his method have at first an unreal sound; the whole operation seems mysteriously or miraculously simple. And yet men and women have been actually healed—not all the cases that present themselves, by any means, but a good many. Formerly such cures might have been called miracles; now they are merely the application of understood scientific methods. Of course the ultimate "Why?" of the healing is as much a mystery as ever it was. Mental healing has been compared to the use of electricity. Although we learn more every year of methods of using the force known as electricity, yet we know nothing whatever concerning the real nature of that force. And thus, though cures are wrought by mental treatment, yet we know nothing of the real nature of the forces which are invoked.

In order to convey an even more vivid idea of the method of treatment, I will give an exact account of it as I saw it in operation. The case in point was one treated by the Rev. Lyman P. Powell of St. John's Church, Northampton, Massachusetts, who has been unusually successful in applying the methods of the

Emmanuel Movement. A tall, rather fine-looking man—Mr. X.—came into the rector's study. He did not look at all ill, but I learned that he had been under treatment for several months. His story was a familiar one. He had come a stranger to the city with his family; he had been under a great strain, he was without acquaintances, and he had begun to use stimulants until he found himself unable to throw off the habit. As a final resort he sought out Mr. Powell.

"If you really want to be cured, I can cure you," said the rector.

"I do want to be cured," said Mr. X.

The treatments began then and there, and Mr. X. reports that he has not since taken to drink. He has, moreover, become a steady attendant with all his family at Mr. Powell's church. He is a wholly different man. On the night I was there Mr. Powell gave him a treatment. The man sat comfortably in an easy chair, the light was turned down, the study was silent and peaceful. Mr. Powell stood behind the chair and told Mr. X. to compose himself, that he was going to sleep just as he had gone to sleep before when he had come to the study.

TREATING A MAN FOR ALCOHOLISM.

"You are going to sleep," said Mr. Powell; "you are sinking deeper into sleep. No noises will disturb you. You will drop off into sleep. You are asleep."

These words, repeated numerous times, soon produced a deep sleep on the part of Mr. X. I could hear his steady slow breathing. Then Mr. Powell began giving suggestions in a low monotone.

"I told you before that you were not to drink any more. I told you that you could not yield again to the drink habit. You cannot drink any more. You will go on now into the perfection of freedom. Your whole physical nature will revolt at the thought of alcohol. If you should take to drink again it would blast your life and leave your wife and children without support; it would cost you your position. You are too good a man to drink; you are too fine a character to be ruined by drink. In God's name I command you

THE SPIRITUAL UNREST

therefore not to drink any more. You cannot drink any more. You will use every means to keep from drink; you will not be able to drink any more."

These suggestions were repeated in different forms many times, the treatment lasting perhaps ten or fifteen minutes. The patient was then aroused. After Mr. X. went away I asked Mr. Powell if his treatment was not in its essence the practice of hypnotism.

"We do not often hypnotize our patients," he said; "it is not necessary. Our idea, of course, is to influence their subconscious lives; to replace their hopelessness and moral weakness with suggestions of power and virtue and strength. We do not need to produce a hypnotic sleep, except in rare cases, to reach this end. All that is required is a relaxation of mind and body, a repose, in which the deeper nature is open to suggestion. We don't know why it is, but if good thoughts and strong purposes are thus impressed upon the mind of a patient in times of repose, these good thoughts act upon and stimulate his life afterward. He is cured, sometimes instantly, of his sick-

HEALING THE SICK

ness or his sin, but usually the treatments must continue for some time."

RELIEVING PAIN.

In some cases organic diseases seem to be incidentally helped or the pain eliminated. I visited one of Mr. Powell's patients who was afflicted with a malignant internal growth and often suffered the most excruciating pain. She had been more or less bedridden for years and had taken all sorts of medicine for relief. Mr. Powell has been treating her now for many months, not promising a cure but merely freedom from suffering. The pain instantly disappears under his treatment so that the patient rests in perfect comfort or is even able to get up and walk. In four or five days, however, the pain returns and Mr. Powell gives another treatment. This summer a remarkable thing happened. Mr. Powell was away on his vacation for several weeks and during a part of the time the woman suffered acutely, but on the day she heard that Mr. Powell was returning so great was her faith in his power to bring relief that the pain stopped before he arrived. He is thus able to make the life of a suffering woman comfortable and even happy where it was formerly wholly miserable.

All sorts of cases have been treated by Dr. Worcester and Dr. McComb and their followers. The lives of many men and women have been utterly transformed; from weak, hopeless, complaining, suffering beings, they have changed to hopeful, happy, courageous beings. In April, 1907, for example, there entered the clinic a middle-aged man suffering from pseudo-angina pectoris, severe psychic pains all over the body, and in a very miserable state of mind. He had been unable to do any work for almost three years, had gone the usual round of doctors and hospitals, and had fallen into despair of getting better. He was a man of deep religious feeling. First of all his despair was dissipated by frequent reassurance that there was nothing incurable about his disorder. Then from time to time during a period of five months suggestion was applied and his religious instincts appealed to, until at the end of that period he recovered his health and nervous balance. He

HEALING THE SICK

has remained well and has gone back to work.

There have been many strange cases of men suffering from fears, worries and phobias which have paralyzed their lives. From all sorts of causes they had come to a nervous breakdown which neither medical treatment nor self-control could cure. They have had their lives in many cases literally reconstructed.

One day after Sunday morning service in the church, Dr. McComb saw a woman leading forward a tall, emaciated, dissipated-looking man.

"Doctor," she said, "you must cure this man."

Dr. McComb said that he was in the midst of his Sunday service and that he could not do anything until Monday.

"But he must be cured," insisted the woman.

Finally Dr. McComb yielded and took the man into his study. It was a case of hopeless alcoholism—in which the man had reached the end of his rope, had ceased to work, neglected his family.

"Do you want to stop drinking?" asked Dr. McComb.

THE SPIRITUAL UNREST

"Yes," said the man.

Beginning then and there, Dr. McComb treated him for several days, and from the first the man has not returned to his evil habits.

But the mere treatment by suggestion is not the only remedy used. Suggestion must be accompanied by education and continuous moral influence. The devil having been cast out, new interests and activities must be inspired, else seven devils will appear to fill the place of the one cast out. Emmanuel Church has an organization of social workers, both paid and voluntary, who follow up the cases treated. For example, the alcoholic, whom I have just mentioned, was visited in his home, money was advanced to buy him a wagon, he was set to work at once making a living and his family was helped and cheered. He is paying back the money loaned to him and getting hold of life again.

HOW AUTO-SUGGESTION IS PRACTICED.

One great effort made by the Emmanuel Movement is to encourage patients in auto-suggestion, that is, in the effort to heal themselves, to give them power over their own na-

HEALING THE SICK

tures. The Rev. Lyman P. Powell has been especially successful in developing the use of auto-suggestion. Having cured himself of persistent insomnia, he gives a clear statement of methods by which other people may do the same thing:

"Those to whom auto-suggestion is an unfamiliar thought sometimes find difficulty in beginning to use it. They need to know how others who have found it helpful in inducing sleep actually use it. The following formula, which has helped several, is given for illustrative purposes. If used audibly it should be said slowly, drowsily, soothingly, whisperingly, and repeated till sleep comes:

"'I am going to sleep. I shall not lie awake. I cannot lie awake. I am going to sleep. The tired eyes are closing. The blood is flowing from my brain to my extremities. There is no longer any pressure on the brain. The muscles are relaxing. Sleep is stealing over all my senses. They are growing numb. I am getting drowsy, drowsy. I am softly sinking into sleep, dreamless sleep. I am sinking deeper, deeper, deeper. I am almost asleep. I am asleep, asleep, asleep.'"

I do not desire to overemphasize the success of the new work. While most patients have been helped, some have received no benefit. There must not only be the power of suggestion on the part of the minister but *faith* on the part of the patient. He must believe and be willing to try and fight. There are dark cases in which character seems to have been entirely broken down; nothing is left to build upon, not even that desire for better things, which is the beginning of faith. Especially difficult have been the cases of men suffering from the drug habit—the use of morphine or cocaine—and yet even these have been helped.

HEALTH SERVICES IN THE CHURCH.

In addition to quiet personal treatment a largely attended meeting is held every Wednesday evening in the church. It is in reality an apotheosis of the old ill-attended prayer-meeting; but under the impetus of the new work, people come by hundreds; there are often eight hundred to one thousand men and women present. After singing and Bible reading requests for prayer are read. "A woman who is to undergo a serious operation

HEALING THE SICK

to-night asks your prayers that she may be sustained." "A man struggling with the demon of drink asks your prayers." These are merely samples. The people kneel and Dr. McComb or Dr. Worcester prays. Afterward a short practical address, applying the teachings of Christ to human ills, is given. When this service is over the people go up to the social room where an hour is spent in making and renewing acquaintances. Many of those who come have had great help from these meetings.

It is difficult to convey any idea of the eagerness with which suffering men and women, Protestants, Catholics, Jews, non-believers, have come to Emmanuel Church, in search of the new life. Where once the ministers were compelled to go out and urge men to come in, it is difficult now to find room or time for all who come. Last winter Dr. Worcester was awakened about four o'clock one morning by a ring at his door-bell. Half aroused, he thought he heard a man crying or groaning. He went to his window and looked out. There, sprawled on his front steps, lay the body of a man. He rushed down and opened the door and found the man lying in his blood, his wrists cut in an attempt to commit suicide. Dr. Worcester sent for a doctor and after the necessary medical treatment found out that the poor fellow was suffering from hypochondria, "life not worth living," and after a number of treatments brought him around all right. The young man told Dr. Worcester he had heard of his work and took a last chance to come from Rhode Island to see if he could not be helped.

People have come not only from Boston but from all over the country, one the other day from Glasgow, Scotland, and the mail received by Dr. Worcester and Dr. McComb is very heavy. Many ministers and doctors have come to study the work; and last spring, so great was the demand, a sort of summer school, or course of lectures, was provided, extending over three weeks' time. A small fee was charged, and many ministers, doctors, teachers and social workers were in attendance. In fact, the movement has spread like wildfire. It has been taken up in churches in New York, Chicago, Kansas City, Buffalo and in many smaller cities.

CRITICISMS OF THE MOVEMENT.

I have thus endeavored to give a clear account of the Emmanuel Movement. What now are the criticisms of it?

The questions I have heard most frequently advanced are these: "Where does religion come in? Cures are made, but how are they different from similar mental cures made by physicians or indeed other persons who know how to practice suggestion? Why should the church enter upon the matter at all?"

Upon these points I have made many inquiries of the ministers and physicians who are interested in the movement and I have also talked with a number of the patients who have been helped. I shall condense their arguments here.

There are two groups of reasons why the church should take up the work of healing. The first is a human or social reason. To be really cured a man must be dealt with not merely as a material body composed of such and such chemical elements, but as a human being, having a soul, a spirit. Man is a religious animal, and any work for his upbuilding that neglects that element neglects the most important factor in his life. Not every doctor is fitted to build up the moral and spiritual nature of men; nor have most doctors time for such work, whereas the minister is more or less at the service of the public.

The sick man, coming for treatment to the church, say the supporters of the movement, receives not mere scientific advice and direction, but what to many sufferers, especially from nervous diseases, is far more important, human sympathy, disinterested advice. To many patients the fact that they are brought out of lonely lives to friendly surroundings, the quieting and hope-inspiring meetings of the church, where everyone is trying to look on the bright side of life, is a powerful stimulant toward health. To this must be added the important matter of confession. Before a patient can be successfully treated he must unburden his soul, must let the minister who is treating him understand to the depths all the sources of his troubles. Without this it is impossible to begin anew, and the very fact that a sufferer can thus unburden himself of his secret troubles and receive sympathetic

HEALING THE SICK

advice and comfort often starts him on his way toward better living. The church inspires confidence that its ministers have no ulterior or selfish purpose; and many a discouraged man finds in that feeling the first gleams of a new hope. Besides this, the church gives men a new interest in life, a new work to do—work for some one beside themselves. Dr. Richard C. Cabot of Boston says of his practice: "I think one-half of all the nervous people who come to me are suffering for want of an outlet. They have been going at half pressure, on half steam, with a fund of energy lying dormant." One of the efforts of the Emmanuel Movement is to get men and women to work, accomplishing something which is unselfishly useful. And in that alone, in many cases, lies a distinct curative power.

But the great influence of the church in healing lies in religious faith. It is spiritual. Dr. Worcester quotes a striking passage from Möbius upon this point:

"We reckon the downfall of religion as one of the causes of mental and nervous disease. Religion is essentially a comforter. It builds for the man who stands amid the misery and evil of the world another and fairer world. Meditation calms and refreshes him like a healing bath. The more religion descends into life the more it remains at man's side early and late, the more it affects our daily life the more powerful is its consoling influence. In proportion as it disappears out of the human life and as the individual and the nation become irreligious, the more comfortless and irritating life becomes."

WHY RELIGION HELPS TO HEAL DISEASE.

A man is not really cured until his character is changed, until he has substituted peace, love and courage, for fear, worry, sin. Physical disease is often only a symptom of deeper distresses of the personality growing out of sin and selfishness, and such a physical disease cannot be permanently cured until the deep underlying cause is removed. And these things are within the gift of religion and religion alone.

"Trust in God," says Dr. McComb, "draws together the scattered forces of the inner life, unifies the dissociations of consciousness cre-

HEALING THE SICK

ated by guilt and remorse, soothes the wild emotions born of sorrow or despair, and touches the whole man to finer issues of peace and power and holiness. By the sweet constraint of such a faith, the jarred and jangled nerves are restored to harmony. The sense of irremediable ill disappears and hope sheds her light once more upon the darkened mind."

But perhaps the best explanation of the need of religion in the healing of the body is given not by a minister but by one of the foremost physicians of Boston—Dr. Cabot. It is noteworthy that while Dr. Cabot is greatly interested in the Emmanuel Movement he is connected with no church. He says in his little book, "Psychotherapy and its Relation to Religion":

"I think I can best make the matter clear by calling your attention to a distinction which I have already used, the distinction between a pain and what we think of it, or between a suffering or a misfortune of any kind and what we think of it. These two elements always exist, are always separable, and in my opinion they are usually to be dealt with by quite different methods. The pain must be dealt with largely by physical methods and by the physician, but what the man thinks of it, that goes down deep into his character, involves the whole mental life, his whole point of view, his religion. It is for this reason that psychotherapy is so directly and deeply connected with religion and needs so constantly the support and guidance of the religious conception of life."

I asked one of the Emmanuel Movement patients, who had been relieved of a serious nervous disease, what part religion played in his case. "Would not a doctor who knew how to give this mental treatment have done as well?" I asked him.

A PATIENT TELLS HOW HE WAS CURED.

"Perhaps," he said, "I hadn't thought of it. I am not a church member or even a churchgoer, or was not before I was cured. But it seemed to me, when I went to the rector for treatment—I was then a perfect stranger to him—that somehow the church guaranteed that I should receive honest advice, that its ministers should tell me the truth. I seemed to get something behind me immediately to

HEALING THE SICK

help me support my weak life. I don't know that I've got any more religion than I ever had; I don't know exactly what religion is; but I do know that I am far sounder in health, that I feel at peace with myself, that I want to live a better all-round life, and as you see, I've developed a passion for telling everybody of the good news about how I was cured. It seems to me that everybody with anything wrong can be cured as I was if I could only let them know about it."

But there are other criticisms levied at the Emmanuel Movement. Some of the physicians, among them Dr. Putnam, who were at first supporters of the movement, now believe that it has gone too far and too fast, that it will escape from the hands of its well-grounded originators and be used by unwise and careless imitators. There is danger, they assert, that the church, without sufficient scientific knowledge, will enter upon the treatment of many people with physical ailments who should be under skilled medical supervision. They say: If the clergymen are to engage in the practical work of healing to the extent indicated, they should organize better for this one end and form a new *institution* analogous to that of the medical profession devoted wholly to the work. This would be undesirable for many reasons and the churches themselves are not ready for it. At the same time able doctors believe that they themselves should be open-minded and that both clergymen and physicians should strengthen each other's position and influence.

Others fear the use of suggestion in untrained hands. In the cure of nervous diseases suggestion is, moreover, only one element, albeit a powerful one; there must also be a steady "re-education" of the patient, a training of his will; an effort, not only to reach him by the "back-door method" of influencing his subconscious self, but to train him in self-control. Can the church do this work satisfactorily; has it the wisdom and knowledge? To these objections the leaders of the Emmanuel Movement reply that any new movement or discovery is likely to go too far or to be used unwisely by over-hasty people. The X-ray treatment, for example, was at first carried much too far, and until the limitations of its use were discovered it injured many peo-

HEALING THE SICK

ple. As to "re-education" and the necessity of long-continued supervision of the patient and the upbuilding of his character, the Emmanuel Movement believes it is better fitted through its many avenues of personal influence and social work to influence the patient and change his life than is the busy, privately paid doctor.

STRUGGLE BETWEEN MINISTERS AND DOCTORS.

Thus, though there is a union of ministers and doctors in the work of the Emmanuel Movement, yet back of it all lies a real struggle of the two professions to attain a greater influence over the lives of men. Both are competing for the new field and the church is not more energetic than the medical profession. For at the same time that the Emmanuel Movement is spreading, a similar work is going on in medicine. An effort is being made to answer the need of medical students for a more extended knowledge of psychology and psychotherapeutics. The University of Wisconsin has established a chair in Psychology and Medicine. The Phipps Fund of $500,000 will shortly be available for a similar course in the University of Pennsylvania, and Dr. Weir Mitchell will throw the weight of his name and personality into its inception. Dr. G. Stanley Hall offers a series of free lectures in the same subject at Clark University this winter, and Professor Morton Prince has started a similar course at Tufts. The doctors have also been scarcely less energetic than the ministers in writing articles and books on various phases of the new healing.

CONCLUSIONS.

Thus while the church asserts the need of more faith in the healing of men, the medical profession demands sounder reason, more scientific insight. Both are necessary; and it is significant of the power of the present spiritual awakening that both doctor and minister should be struggling to fill this newly recognized need of human life. It would seem that the only way out was for the medical profession to become more religious and the ministry more scientific. Both faith and reason are needed; but the one most difficult to cherish and keep alive is faith, religious faith. Without faith we are dead; we do not grow. It i

HEALING THE SICK

easy enough to give reasons why the fire of faith, such as that kindled by the Emmanuel Movement, does not or should not burn; it is more difficult to kindle and keep alive that precious fire.

In the final analysis it makes little real difference to you or to me what profession does the new work—whether doctor or minister or a combination of the two—so long as it is done. The final test is service, and to that end institutions and professions must shape themselves. Men, after all, whether ill or well, will follow those leaders who can give them hope, courage, faith, health, virtue, enable them to meet the inevitable difficulties and trials of this life with a happier face and a serener soul. In any event the fine new work will go on, whether the church in its present form leads it or not, for that way lies truth.

CHAPTER VI

THE FAITH OF THE UNCHURCHED: INSPIRATIONS FROM OUT SIDE THE CHURCH

I HAVE spoken in previous chapters of the vitality of some of the social and philanthropic work outside of the churches. Always in times of readjustment, institutional lines grow lax, and impulses and inspirations come from many sources. Some of the most striking of these outside activities have wholly departed from any church influence and not a few are not openly religious, though truly religious, in their results.

Among the chief of these unchurched activities I should class the social settlement movement, hospital extension, municipal and political reform, and many of the newer forms of charity and education. All these movements represent the faith, however groping, however unconscious, of the unchurched, or of those who, though still nominally connected

FAITH OF THE UNCHURCHED

with the churches, find the most satisfactory avenues for the expression of their religious idealism in organizations outside of the churches.

THE STORY OF HUDSON GUILD.

Perhaps I can best convey what I mean by the "faith of the unchurched" by a concrete example of an expression of this faith. I want to tell here of the work of the Hudson Guild of New York City.

Dr. John Lovejoy Elliott, the organizer and leader of the Hudson Guild movement, has been for many years associated with Dr. Felix Adler of the Ethical Culture Society. A man of the broadest and kindliest human sympathies, he wished to see the principles he taught in the Ethical Culture school worked out in the hard laboratory of everyday life. He chose one of the most difficult fields in the city, the tenement district of the west side of Manhattan Island, and there he has lived for nearly fifteen years.

During the past quarter century the social settlement movement has been the direct reverse of the church movement. While the tendency of the churches, especially the Protestant churches, has been to fly from the tenements, the social settlements have taken root among the poorest of the poor without regard to religious belief. And while the church in the large cities has lost ground both in attendance and influence, the social settlements have flourished marvelously. Though the movement is scarcely twenty-five years old, there are to-day in New York City about seventy-five social settlements, with hundreds of residents and workers. Some of them are provided with costly buildings and are doing an extraordinary work. The influence of leaders like Miss Wald of the Nurses' Settlement, Gaylord S. White, Miss Williams, Mrs. Simkhovitch and many others upon the life of the city has been noteworthy. In Chicago Miss Addams has been called the "most useful citizen." It can be said with truth that the only Protestant churches to-day in the poorer parts of the city of New York which are enjoying any success at all are winning it because they have adopted in greater or less degree the settlement idea.

What is the idea of the social settler? It is

primarily to give himself in service; to live among the people, to know them and touch them intimately, and to help them without trying to teach any specific religious doctrine.

HOW THE "UPPER HALF" HAS COME TO KNOW THE "UNDER HALF."

For a number of years settlement work consisted merely of living among and getting acquainted with the "other half," with a resulting spread of information concerning the "under half" among the "upper half." I need scarcely call attention to the extraordinary spread of knowledge which has come to us during the past dozen years of the life of the tenements, of the ways and needs of the foreign emigrant, of sweat-shops and child labor, of corrupt politics in its relationships to the poor. Much of this knowledge was the outcome of the humble desire of devoted men and women, not to proselyte their neighbors, but to know them and to serve them.

That was the first stage. Upon it and out of it is slowly forming a wonderful new movement, chaotic and dim as yet in the further reaches of its vision, but every month becoming surer of itself. It may be seen developing in Chicago in the work of Miss Addams, Professor Taylor, Miss McDowell, Jenkin Lloyd Jones and others, and in New York in the activities of many of the settlements. I describe here the work of Hudson Guild not because it is better than the work of several other settlements, but because it has articulated itself with clearness and has introduced a number of significant democratic features.

No leadership is genuine unless based upon thorough knowledge and complete sympathy. Tammany Hall has been so long and so violently attacked for its evil deeds that many people have lost the significance of its long-continued survival and its repeated victories. Tammany Hall has succeeded because its leaders knew the people and sympathized with them. It knew how to direct that instinct of men—which is pretty nearly the deepest instinct of all—of association—the "gang spirit" if you will. It did not matter that the Tammany leadership was evil as looked at from above, for it appeared to be human and helpful, as looked at from below.

But in recent years the social settler has

come to know the "other half" as well as Tammany Hall—better, indeed, for its knowledge is the outgrowth of unselfish sympathy. Having thus come to understand the people, leadership was sure to follow. And that leadership, inspired with a fine and sturdy idealism, is now making itself felt. It is the beginning of a new and wonderful era in our life.

HOW DR. ELLIOTT BEGAN HIS WORK.

When Dr. Elliott began his work fourteen years ago he did exactly what Tammany does: he organized a club of boys and young men. He has the sort of genuis that the Tammany Hall politicians possess—a genius for being friendly and helpful, a genius for inspiring and directing association among men.

Out of that first club grew other clubs, first with rented quarters and no especial work to do outside of the ordinary social and semi-literary activities which occupied so exclusively the attention of the earlier settlement workers. The leader had to feel his way, gain knowledge of people and conditions, learn how to make his followers act from motives of social helpfulness rather than from motives of immediate selfish aggrandizement. He must make his followers see further than the immediate job, or the immediate favor which Tammany offered. Yet he must begin, humbly enough, not with what he wants, but with what the people want—the daily job and the evening amusement, and out of those common things he must build up higher wants and inspire better desires.

Two years ago the work had grown so promising that a fine brick building, five stories high, was constructed in West Twenty-seventh Street in the midst of a swarming population of Irish-Americans, Italians and Jews. While the larger part of the money for the building was supplied by well-to-do people uptown who were interested through Dr. Elliott in the work, it is significant that several thousand dollars was contributed directly by the people of the neighborhood who had become interested in the clubs. I know of no other case where the working people of a neighborhood have contributed any considerable sum of money to such a building.

Three things attracted me especially when

FAITH OF THE UNCHURCHED

I first visited Hudson Guild. The first was its masculine cast. It is difficult to attract grown men either to churches or settlements. Hudson Guild is full of men. The second thing that impressed me was the resemblance of the Guild to an ordinary uptown club. With its meeting rooms, its baths, its gymnasium, its library, its music, it had the air of free association of a real club. The third thing that impressed me was the fact that the Guild seemed to be running itself. The first afternoon I went there I found plenty of young men and boys, besides a roomful of girls, but no "leaders" or "workers" except the librarian. Later I discovered the workers, but, compared with many settlements, they are few in numbers.

A GUILD THAT RUNS ITSELF.

I soon discovered that not only does the Guild give an appearance of running itself, but that it really *does* run itself. That is the marvel of it. The one essential purpose of education is to set an individual to going from within; to start his machinery so that he will run himself.

THE SPIRITUAL UNREST

The same end must be sought with institutions: an institution is never really successful until it goes of itself, impelled by the life within. No matter how joltingly it operates, no matter how painful the noise it makes, if it really runs from within, there is something creative, something immortal about it.

Hudson Guild runs itself—joltingly yet, with a push now and then from a helpful hand, but it really runs. Over fifty diffcrent clubs and other organizations now find the center of their social life at the Guild. All of them are made up exclusively of working people of the Chelsea district, largely Irish-Americans, with some Italians and Jews. Each of these clubs is an independent, self-governing body, which elects delegates to a general or federal Council—a sort of congress which meets once a month. I attended one of the meetings. About sixty delegates were present, half men and boys, and half women and girls. This Council conducts the business of the Guild—*really* conducts it, because it has to pay a large part of the running expenses of the work. Each club pays a regular tax or rental into the common treasury, amounting last year to over $1,800—a good deal of money for such a group of working people. Out of this sum the Council pays for lighting, heating, repairs and janitor service of the building. All of the details of management are in the hands of a house committee elected by the Council. The chairman of this house committee at present is Wm. T. Farrell, a bricklayer by trade, who has been identified with the clubs of the Guild since he was a boy. He is on hand nearly every evening, and both he and all other members of the Council committees, though their duties require a good deal of time and attention, serve wholly without compensation. It is a real thing with them, in which they are vitally interested.

The Council also has charge of assignments of rooms to the various clubs, it dictates what entertainments shall be given and at what times, decides disputes between clubs and directs in large measure the sort of educational work to be undertaken.

A single club belonging to the Council, the Athletic Association, has 800 members. This organization not only pays its rentals but has

THE SPIRITUAL UNREST

largely outfitted the gymnasium, paid the operating expenses, and financed the baseball and track teams from its own treasury.

When people have to pay for things they look after them, therefore the Guild efficiently safeguards itself—like any club. If property is injured the members know that they will have to pay for it. Dr. Elliott tells how the house committee has reprimanded him more than once for leaving his electric lights burning.

Dr. Elliott, of course, is the leader and headworker and yet he submits himself to the rules of the Guild. Under the constitution he may even be impeached. Here is the section:

Sec. 2.—The Council may at any time by a two-thirds vote impeach the Headworker and it shall be the duty of the president of the Council to announce to the Council the next regular meeting of the Board of Trustees, when delegates shall be appointed to lay the matter at issue between the Council and the Headworker before the Board of Trustees.

"The best thing that we can do for self-government," says Dr. Elliott, "is not to interfere with it too much."

FAITH OF THE UNCHURCHED

A great variety of activities is constantly under way at the Guild, Dr. Elliott's idea being that moral education comes through activity, that the way to displace evil activities is by encouraging better activities.

The clubs of the Guild are therefore constantly organizing and conducting dances, giving plays, festivals and smokers, organizing track and field sports, supporting strong baseball and basket-ball teams. More than this, the Guild aims to help fit its members for better work: it has classes for those who wish to enter the civil service, and carpentry and cooking classes. A print-shop not only trains boys in the printing art and does all the printing for the Guild, including the publication of a monthly newspaper, but enough outside pay work has been secured to meet nearly all of its running expenses. One of the enterprises of the Guild is a bank which receives deposits and pays interest to the members. One of the young clubmen, a bookkeeper by occupation, is the chosen banker.

Of course not all of the work by any means is voluntary. The Guild, like social settlements generally, has a number of paid workers, paid by a group of people uptown who have long been interested in the work. One of Dr. Elliott's assistants is John Splain, who was a boy of the neighborhood, trained in the first club organized by Dr. Elliott. He learned the printer's trade, but finally gave up a good position to come with Dr. Elliott. His mother desired him to be a priest; now she contents herself with saying that "he is doing the work of a priest without taking orders." Born in the neighborhood, married there, and living there, his knowledge of the people make him a valuable helper. Other workers include Mrs. Hohoff, district visitor; Miss Wolff, chairman of the district committee, and Miss Westcott, who is connected with the women's and girls' clubs; Mr. Gleason, who has charge of the gymnasium, four kindergarten teachers, a librarian, a visiting nurse and a master printer.

Dr. Elliott gives close personal attention to the clubs. He and John Splain meet with the clubs, discuss various subjects with them or tell stories which illustrate ethical truths. Story-telling is, indeed, one of the chief methods of instruction which they employ.

FAITH OF THE UNCHURCHED

Most of the activities so far described are more or less common to many settlements, though none that I know of has reached the degree of self-government, self-direction and self-support here attained. But the Guild has made a step far in advance of this—a very remarkable new step. Not only is the Guild interested in developing and amusing its own members, but it is animated with a spirit of what may be called neighborhood consciousness. As a center for social activities it is beginning to feel a responsibility for all the life around it.

INSPIRING A CITY NEIGHBORHOOD.

Quite the most interesting thing to me about the Council meeting which I attended was not merely the fact that it was self-governing, but that it was *using its self-governed organization for the benefit of the whole neighborhood*. That is a great step in advance. Let me give some examples of what the Council did on the night I attended its meeting.

A small park has been established by the city upon the block across the street from the Guild. All the tenements have been torn down and plans have been made for improving the land. The young men of the Guild thought that a running track and other facilities for athletics should be provided in the park, but the park department had demurred. The Council therefore appointed a committee to wait on the proper officials to see if such facilities could not be provided.

Another committee was appointed to work with the citizens' movement against the granting of a franchise to the New York Central Railroad Company to continue its tracks in Eleventh Avenue. At this meeting there was also some talk of the condition of the tenements. Members were urged to make complaints, so that the attention of the board of health or the tenement house department could be called to conditions. One of the members objected that if complaints were made and landlords were forced to improve their buildings that they would raise the rents.

"And," he said, "we are paying all the rent now that we can afford to pay."

In short, they struck down in this discussion, upon fundamental living problems of the neighborhood and of tenement house people.

In another way the Guild is developing a neighborhood consciousness. Patterning after Tammany Hall a district committee has been formed with a captain in every block. Sometimes this captain is a small storekeeper, sometimes a woman well known in her tenement. These captains keep watch of things generally, report unsanitary tenements, or find cases of tuberculosis or contagion. All this is reported to the Guild and a district visitor is sent out to investigate. Thus the whole neighborhood is coming into touch with the Guild, and an interest in improving the neighborhood is being developed. The work is new yet and feeble, but it lives and grows. In many instances people ill with tuberculosis have been sent away to the sanitarium and all their expenses met by the clubs of the Guild—not as charity but as a sort of neighborhood duty.

Let me give one example. In November, 1907, a member reported that a girl named Alice Smith (not her true name) in one of the tenements was ill with tuberculosis. Two of the oldest clubs of the Guild got together and raised $50 and sent the girl to the sanitarium at Liberty, N. Y. Afterward they kept in touch with her, assessed themselves regularly, paid all her expenses, and now at the end of two years she is discharged, cured, and is making her own living. In the week I last visited the Guild two other patients were sent away, the expenses of one being largely met by one of the afternoon boys' clubs.

Last year the work of the district committee cost $750 and nearly all of this sum was supplied, not from any outside source, but by the clubs themselves. A basket-ball contest held by the clubs yielded $110 for the purpose; the Mothers' Club raised $120, and a collection at one of the men's smokers for a special case brought in $45.

All this work is most significant. It is a fine thing to help a girl with tuberculosis to freedom from her disease, it is fine to improve a miserable tenement-house, but it is finer, far finer, to develop the active social and neighborhood spirit which does the work. So much social work at the present time is just work,

FAITH OF THE UNCHURCHED

with no social feeling or social spirit behind it. The war on tuberculosis is not the *end* of social work, but should be rather a *means* for awakening the spirit of democracy among men.

Here will be found the difference between the institutional work of many churches and that of Hudson Guild. In the case of the churches, rich men supply the money, workers are hired and everything is directed from above and from without. This is the reason for the distressing failure of so much of the work of the churches. They are not really willing to trust the people with religion; they have no faith in people. They do not realize that an institution does not exist to dominate people but to serve people. That is the reason why I have made such a point of the fact that Hudson Guild *runs* itself from power generated within itself. It is a tremendous thing when a group of working men and women begin to take pride in their own surroundings, and are willing to contribute their own money and their own time to improving them. And once started the spirit grows wonderfully. It is like an ever-expanding whirlpool to which the right impetus has been given.

"NOTHING SO CATCHING AS A GOOD ACT."

"Nothing," says Dr. Elliott, "is so catching as a good act."

A great city distracts people, crushes individuals. Hudson Guild strives to awaken a neighborhood interest, a neighborhood self-consciousness. The monthly journal of the Guild is called *Chelsea,* Chelsea being the old name of the neighborhood, and it is filled, not with city news, but with news of the people of the neighborhood, the parks of the neighborhood, the ball games of the neighborhood, the dances of the neighborhood—everything to interest the people in the common life and activities of Chelsea.

Hudson Guild is thus genuinely getting hold of and organizing the people. It is a sort of town-hall for the neighborhood. In a former chapter I quoted Paul Sabatier on the character of the Middle Age cathedrals. Says M. Sabatier:

"The cathedrals were the lay churches of the thirteenth century. Built by the people for the people, they were originally the true common house of our old cities. Museums, granaries, chambers of commerce, halls of justice, depositories of archives and even labor exchanges, they were all these at once."

In some degree institutions like Hudson Guild in New York and Hull House in Chicago are approaching the idea of the old cathedrals; in that they are the "common houses" the "lay churches" of our modern cities. They are animated by a catholicity of spirit, a passion for service, and a faith in people which cannot but give one a new confidence in the future of his country.

Hudson Guild is only one example or expression of what I have called the "faith of the unchurched." Let us look into some other manifestations of it.

One of the deepest, most complex, most dangerous of the problems of our times is that of poverty. What shall be done for the millions who live along the poverty line or below, who fill the tenements, who recruit the ranks of the unemployed? For a thousand years—always, in fact—the church has been facing the problem of poverty. Almsgiving has been one of the bulwarks of church work, and so it continues to be to this day. The church has ever been a mediator between rich and poor; asking of the rich to keep the poor from suffering. And always the church has acquiesced in poverty. It has quoted Scripture: "the poor ye have always with you" and it has acted upon that statement by doling out help, here a little, there a little. It has palliated and soothed; the poor have been kept content with the promise that patience in bearing poverty and toil and injustice while other people enjoy unearned wealth and luxury, will win the devout soul the bliss of a distant heaven—after death.

It will be objected that many churches no longer make these promises of a distant heaven, or utter threats of a hell; but it is a significant fact that those churches which promise and threaten least, the Unitarian and Congregational, for example, are thriving least, while those which still promise and threaten most: the Roman Catholics and the Methodists, for example, are best holding their own.

And no one, for an instant, would deny that

FAITH OF THE UNCHURCHED

it has been a great and useful and necessary work to comfort the afflicted and help the poor; nor that the church has been diligent at it. But while the church has continued at the negative work of palliation and promise, many people outside of the churches have had a new vision; they have seen a new light; whole groups of men and women are to-day on fire with the new faith that poverty can be *abolished*, that in a land which produces more than enough to keep every man, woman and child in comfort, it is absurd that millions should suffer from want at one end of the social ladder while thousands should decay with luxury and superfluity at the other end.

WHY PEOPLE ARE INTERESTED IN SOCIALISM.

Why are many people interested in Socialism? Because the Socialists have seen this vision; and they have a faith in it that prompts men to work and to sacrifice. I am not arguing that the Socialists are right either in their program or their methods; I am calling attention to the brightness of their vision and the power of the faith which it animates. I have attended meetings of Socialists in New

York at which I saw men and women of half a dozen nationalities, three races, and I don't know how many shades of religious belief—but they were all here united in a common faith. While religion still divides men into warring camps, the world is discovering that men's interests, social and otherwise, are identical.

And this vision is by no means confined to the Socialists. Probably there are no more cautious or scientific students of social conditions in New York City than the men behind the Charity Organization Society. They have a broad outlook and sound experience. They know better than any other agency the length and breadth and depth of the problem of poverty and yet while the churches are moving out of the slums, and the ministers express discouragement over the conditions, the Charity Organization Society strikes a high note of faith, and is buckling down to the task of producing results. In the 1907 year book I find these words:

"Belief in the possibility of eliminating poverty had not been formulated in so many words as a working motive in the early years, but methods and projects were tested by their probable power to rescue, and not merely to soothe those who are in danger of lapsing into perpetual pauperism. . . . In recent years the growing conviction that not only professional pauperism but unwholesome poverty as well . . . may be obliterated, has almost come to be a fundamental article of faith."

CAN POVERTY BE ABOLISHED?

Such an article of faith is like a trumpet call to all that is heroic and poetic in the souls of men.

Another world problem is that of sickness. What shall be done with people who suffer from disease? Jesus healed people; but the modern churches, for the most part, have no faith in the healing of the body. They will comfort and pray over the sick, they will mourn with the afflicted, but if anyone suggested that the disease which caused the sickness be abolished, they might be, or might have been a few years ago, astonished, if not shocked.

Not so, however, with many people outside

the churches. They have a greater faith. Medical men have declared that the most destructive of all diseases—tuberculosis—can be abolished, and having so expressed their vision, they have straightway begun to transmute faith into works.

A NEW FAITH FOR CURING DISEASE.

One Sunday morning, the sixth of December, I went to see the tuberculosis exhibit in the American Museum of Natural History. It was thronged with people; on that day 43,713 persons visited the exhibit. And as I circulated among those throngs—Protestants, Catholics, Jews, rich and poor—and talked with many people—I seemed to feel a great surge of faith in the possibilities of a newer, finer, sweeter life in New York City. Without creed, or doctrine, or church edifice, I felt that here, indeed, was the true spirit of religion. It may have been blind, but it was big, big; and later its blindness will pass away. One of the test questions of any true religion is this: "Who is my brother?" and here among a score of elbowing races and national-

FAITH OF THE UNCHURCHED

ities, of rich and poor, I caught the grandest of grand answers.

When the problem of municipal corruption arose for solution, the churches, almost without exception, raised no voice, had no faith. Study the reform movements in the cities of America, and it will be found that the regenerative activities have usually been led by men outside of the churches—men inspired with a faith in a God who wanted honest government, and well-paved streets, as well as large churches and singing and prayer. Tenement-house reform in New York has found a bitter enemy in Trinity Church. Here and there bold churchmen like Dr. Parkhurst or Dr. Peters have led valiant fights, but they have done it because their faith was greater than that of their churches. Here is what Frank Moss, one of the leaders of the reform movement in New York, said to a group of clergymen:

"I call you to witness, friends! Has the Christian Church, has the Hebrew Church, has any church, in these days of vice, in these days of crime that have cursed the city, and from which we hope we have been delivered, in these days of shame and degradation—has any church raised its voice of protest? Has any adequate rallying cry gone out from the churches? When the time came to fight the organized corruption that had seized the governmental powers and stolen young men and women right from the very doors of the church; when the time came for a fight we had to turn to politicians to organize and lead the fight. The church was practically dumb."

ANSWER OF THE CHURCHES TO CRITICISMS.

To these criticisms church leaders reply that it is not the business of the churches to go into specific reforms, but to inspire men, to deliver the true message of religion, to save souls.

But what happens if men will not come to be inspired? The churches find it notoriously difficult to get audiences, even with all manner of attractions, brilliant preaching, fine music, costly and beautiful architecture. Not even at revivals—in New York, at least—can the churches find an opportunity to deliver

FAITH OF THE UNCHURCHED

their message to waiting and enthusiastic crowds.

In short, the new faith of the unchurched is a faith in people, in the coming of the kingdom of heaven on earth.

CHAPTER VII

A VISION OF THE NEW CHRISTIANITY—

AN ACCOUNT OF PROFESSOR WALTER RAUSCHENBUSCH AND HIS WORK.

"A MAN was walking through the woods in springtime. The air was thrilling and throbbing with the passion of little hearts, with the love-wooing, the parent pride, and the deadly fear of the birds. But the man never noticed that there was a bird in the woods. He was a botanist and was looking for plants.

"A man was walking through the streets of a city, pondering the problems of wealth and national well-being. He saw a child sitting on a curbstone and crying. He met children at play. He saw a young mother with her child and an old man with his grandchild. But it never occurred to him that little children are the foundation of society, a chief motive power in economic effort, the most influential teachers, the source of the purest pleasures, the embodiment of form and color and grace. The man had never had a child and his eyes were not opened.

"A man read through the New Testament. He felt no vibration of social hope in the preaching of John the Baptist and in the shout of the crowd when Jesus entered Jerusalem. He caught no revolutionary note in the Book of Revelations. The social movement had not yet reached him. Jesus knew human nature when he reiterated: 'He that hath ears to hear, let him hear.'"—*Walter Rauschenbusch.*

THE NEW CHRISTIANITY

If it were possible to sum up in a few words the one thing that has most impressed me in visiting churches and talking with church leaders in various parts of the country, I think I should say:

"The utter confusion of counsel among church leaders themselves."

Upon the seriousness of the crisis which confronts them—the waning influence of the church upon the lives of men and women, the tendency of able young men to avoid the ministry as a profession—most church leaders are quite in agreement, but as to what to do about it, there exist the widest differences of opinion. The church to-day is like a fort under sudden attack—in the night, with many of the captains fast asleep. There is a common and overwhelming sense of danger, but the defense so far has been without common plan or purpose—sallies here, retreats there, a promiscuous firing of big and little guns, and an altogether inordinate amount of noise.

CHURCH-SAVING EXPERIMENTS.

Several groups of churches, chiefly in the Middle West, under the spirited if spectacular leadership of men of the type of Billy Sunday, have dashed into Revivalism, and by means of the old-fashioned emotionalism of the evangelist have stemmed for the moment the tide of attack. On the other hand, certain churches, especially in the East, have been slowly retreating toward the citadel of Authority. At Boston I found Dr. Worcester, now the leader of a considerable number of church workers, advancing Emmanuelism to counteract the steady encroachment of Christian Science and the New Thought, which have been beguiling away many of those who formerly marched under the banner of the old churches. And wherever I have gone I have found a still larger and more active group of leaders absorbed in building new outworks—parish houses and gymnasiums, bowling alleys and clubrooms, carpenter shops, shooting galleries and dance halls—to counteract or at least to parallel the advance of the Social Settlement idea and the expansion of function of the public schools and other municipal institutions. Never before in history, perhaps, was there such a variety of church-saving experiments going forward; and never a more

THE NEW CHRISTIANITY

evident lack of a commanding voice of prophecy, or a generally accepted plan of campaign.

And yet it would be a decided mistake to say that the present day is without its real prophets or that their voices are not beginning to be heard above the turmoil and confusion of the times. One of the questions I have asked most diligently as I have gone about among the more progressive religious leaders of the country is this:

MOST INFLUENTIAL RECENT RELIGIOUS BOOK.

"What recent book, or what man, has given you the most light?"

By all odds the book most frequently mentioned was "Christianity and the Social Crisis," by Walter Rauschenbusch. No recent religious book, perhaps, has had a more favorable reception among both church and secular journals, or a wider reading among religious leaders than this.

It will help us, then, to a clear understanding of one of the strongest currents of thought among religious people both inside and outside of the churches if we can meet Professor Rauschenbusch face to face and ask him what his message is—ask him what, in his opinion, the trouble is with the churches, and what to do about it. For his judgment deserves attention not merely by virtue of a wide approval of his book by thinking men and women, but by right of a thoroughgoing scholarship, a ripe experience in human affairs, and a strong position within the church itself.

Every prophet comes out of the wilderness to speak to men. Professor Rauschenbusch found his message amid obscurity and enforced silence. His poverty gave him freedom and a close touch with the common life. His deafness encouraged that concentration and reflection which busy and popular men usually lack. When his book was published two years ago, he was forty-six years old and little known outside of a narrow circle of devoted friends. His life outwardly has been devoid of notable events. He comes of a family of German Lutherans, and his ancestors for six successive generations have been ministers of the Protestant Church, some of them men of marked ability and character. One of his ancestors was imprisoned for his

THE NEW CHRISTIANITY

faith, and his father, a typical German scholar of the old school, a student of Neander, the great church historian, migrated to America some seventy years ago to preach the gospel among the Germans of this country. Here he broke with the Lutheran Church, and at a serious sacrifice to himself became a Baptist, afterward occupying a professor's chair in the German department of the Baptist Theological Seminary of Rochester, N. Y.

At Rochester the son Walter was born. Under the severe discipline of his father, he received a thoroughgoing education both in America and in Germany. Graduated from the Rochester Theological Seminary in 1886 with a brilliant record, and at the head of his class, he chose to devote himself to religious work among the Germans. He became pastor of a small, struggling German Baptist church on the West Side of New York City, where for eleven years he served a swarming population of wage-working men and women.

When increasing deafness and growing intellectual hunger caused him to relinquish his pastoral work, he accepted a repeated call to a professorship at the Rochester Theological

Seminary, and there he has remained ever since, occupying in recent years the chair of church history. Outside of a "Life of Jesus" and two other small books, all in German, he published nothing of moment until his work, "Christianity and the Social Crisis," appeared two years ago.

INTELLECTUAL EVOLUTION OF A LIBERAL SCHOLAR.

Such, in brief, are the outward facts relating to Professor Rauschenbusch's life. The inner facts, because they mark so plainly the path followed by many progressive thinkers of to-day, are of far greater significance. When he entered the theological seminary, at the age of twenty-two, Professor Rauschenbusch says that he "believed everything"; he believed the Bible to be infallible in every word; his sole aim was to save souls; social questions did not exist for him. The first of the prophets of the new time to influence him was Henry George, whose "Progress and Poverty" set his mind to working in a wholly new field of thought. Arriving in New York at the very time that Henry George was candidate for the mayoralty, he became still more deeply interested. Soon afterward Bellamy's "Looking Backward" touched his imagination with a new social vision and Tolstoi led him to interpret anew the life of Jesus.

"I never understood the Sermon on the Mount," he says, "until I read Tolstoi's 'My Religion.'"

Another book which later influenced him greatly was Mazzini's "Essays," with its passionate teaching of faith as a fundamental need of the people.

During all of the years of his reading, which was extensive and thorough, the hard surroundings of his pastorate, the life of the working people, the congestion of the tenements, the unequal struggle with vice fostered by economic conditions, were giving him visible daily demonstration of the dire need of a new religious impulse and a new social message. He preached steadily, he wrote industriously for both German and American religious journals, he raised money to build a new church, he organized institutional activities, always applying his thinking to the hard realities of the life which surrounded him.

No one can read his book without feeling within it the throb of sympathy and the saving touch of humor that comes only from close contact with the deeper life of our common humanity.

"Those of us," he says, concerning his pastorate, "who passed through the last industrial depression will never forget the procession of men out of work, out of clothes, out of shoes and out of hope. They wore down our threshold, and they wore away our hearts."

Again he says: "During the great industrial crisis of the '90's, I saw good men go into disreputable lines of employment and respectable widows consent to live with men who would support them and their children. One could hear human virtue cracking and crumbling all around."

No mere scholar could have written "Christianity and the Social Crisis"; but on the other hand, no man who was not a scholar could have brought to the common experiences of life such an understanding spirit. And this is what makes the book so convincing—this, and the personality of the man himself which illuminates every page.

THE NEW CHRISTIANITY

PERSONALITY OF PROFESSOR RAUSCHENBUSCH.

A tall, spare man, with a humorous twinkle in his eyes, you may see him walking down to the Seminary in the morning from his home in Shepard Street. Though much occupied with his studies and his classes, he yet finds time for active interest in the affairs of his city and his neighborhood; and he occupies his spare moments at a working bench with a set of wood-carving tools. And never at any time does he yield to the "scholar's fault" of avoiding warm human contact with those about him. Even though his associates do not follow him in all of his views, his personal qualities, his humor and his broad sympathies have bound them all to him. His hold upon his students is profound; he not only opens their hearts, but he liberates their minds. Church history, as ordinarily taught, is about as dry a subject as could well be imagined; but it is not so in Professor Rauschenbusch's class. I attended one of his lectures. It treated of the beginnings of the Protestant Reformation, and so packed was it with modern applications that it was like listening to a luminous and lively account of contemporary politics. In the past, church history has been written and taught almost wholly from an ecclesiastical point of view; everything turned upon what was good or bad for the church as an institution. Professor Rauschenbusch considers it from a far wider view point, as a history of the kingdom of God upon earth. Of each event he asks: Was it good for humanity, how did it affect all the people?

During the last two years Professor Rauschenbusch has lectured somewhat widely in the East; and last year in Germany he delivered an address on the drinking habits of the Germans as seen through American eyes which in pamphlet form has since circulated by thousands of copies. In debate or in the give and take of an after-discussion, he has a quickness and humor of repartee which endears him to every audience.

A rare spirit, indeed, is this deaf prophet of Rochester. His intellect, which is at once keen and deep, with an outlook as lively and sane and sweet as it is lofty, is animated with a glowing religious spirit.

"Love, money and honor are fairest in the

THE NEW CHRISTIANITY

distance," he says. "It does not seem to be so with religious joy; the less so, the more purely religious it is. It does contain the desire for new and larger experiences, but not because the old have palled. There is no unrest in it. The expression 'I have found peace' is, of course, a stock expression, but it does express what is the overwhelming personal feeling in first entering into religious joy. It seems to be the universal testimony of those who have made personal test of it that the joy of religious satisfaction is beyond anything else that life holds."

A BOOK ON SOCIAL CONDITIONS WITH NO HATRED IN IT.

A truly religious spirit, he draws all sorts of men to him, making a sure place in their hearts. Though he writes strongly of social conditions, though his convictions are deep, nowhere in his book will there be found a note of hatred; and he leaves the reader inspired with a new faith in the power of religion to meet and solve the most complex of the problems of the day.

"When politicians and social exploiters,"

he says, "have to deal with the stubborn courage of men who pray about their politics, they will have a new factor to reckon with."

ESSENCE OF PROFESSOR RAUSCHENBUSCH'S MESSAGE.

The essence of Professor Rauschenbusch's message is that religion has not one, but two great functions to perform.

"There are two great entities in human life—the human soul and the human race—and religion is to save both. The soul is to seek righteousness and eternal life; the race is to seek righteousness and the kingdom of God."

In the past, he believes, the churches have concerned themselves too exclusively with personal salvation—the saving of individuals; they have lacked social vision. He believes that the church has now arrived at a stage in its development where it is fit and free for a new social mission and a new evangelism; that, indeed, there must soon come "either a revival of social religion or the deluge." He thinks that civilization to-day is at one of the great crises of its development, and that the

THE NEW CHRISTIANITY

church must awaken to the gravity of conditions or go down to ruin.

A large part of his book is devoted to a scholarly exposition of the distinctly social spirit of Christianity as expressed by the Hebrew prophets and later and still more positively by Jesus. Following this new historical interpretation of the Bible, he gives a graphic picture of present-day social conditions in America, holding them up as both irreligious and immoral. He shows that large numbers of people in this country are in want and poverty at the very time when wealth is accumulating as never before.

"The economic system which produces such injustice," he says, "with the contrasts resulting between Plenty and Want, is in stark contradiction to the spirit of Christianity, and either the one or the other must give way."

He then shows, in a chapter which he regards as his most valuable contribution to religious history, why the churches have never hitherto undertaken to carry out the work of social reconstruction which is the fundamental purpose of Christianity; and he declares that they must, if they would survive, radically change their methods.

WHAT THE CHURCHES SHOULD DO.

Having thus diagnosed present-day conditions, Professor Rauschenbusch's final chapter, entitled, "What to Do," deals with the remedies which in his opinion must be adopted. He believes that the wages system, child-labor, the problem of the ownership or control of public utilities, the military spirit, the labor problem, instead of being beyond the purview of religion, are wholly within the scope of Christian teaching, and that the religious leader must have a message and a prophecy to deliver regarding them.

"What right," he asks, "have Christian ministers to back away from these questions and refuse to contribute whatever moral discernment God has given them?"

In the past the emphasis of preaching and teaching has been upon the repentance of the individual and personal salvation; and the salvation of human personalities must always be one of the great aims of religion.

"Every man is interested in his own soul,"

says Professor Rauschenbusch; "we should show lack of love if we regarded any human being as unimportant."

But there must be, from now forward, quite a new preaching and teaching—the preaching of repentance from social sin and the need of social salvation. The old evangelism fixed the attention of a man upon himself, a selfish saving of himself from hell; the new evangelism fixes his attention equally upon the other man—upon the salvation and reconstruction of human society.

In my conversation with Professor Rauschenbusch I endeavored to draw out just what he meant by the "new evangelism" and what, in his opinion, the future of the churches in this country would be.

THE NEW EVANGELISM.

The new evangelism is made up of the same elements as the old; first, it seeks to convict men of sin; second, to reconstruct their lives. But the conception of both sin and reconstruction in the new evangelism is immensely broader and deeper than in the old. It is as wide as humanity, with a vision and a message calculated to fire the souls of men as nothing in the past has ever fired them.

The new evangelism greatly intensifies our conception of sin. It shows how impossible it is to sin any sin that does not pass along to others. It shows how all men are linked together, and that the sin of one injures all, so that each man realizes that he is involved in the whole sin of mankind.

I asked Professor Rauschenbusch for specific instances as to how the conviction of social sin might be brought about. He gave me as a single example the problem of the wage-worker.

"An idle woman living in wasteful luxury," he said, "wants more beautiful clothing, more jewelry. She has no thought of what her selfish wastefulness may cost. In order to get it her husband pinches his workingmen to the lowest possible wage. Let us say that one of these workingmen has a sick child, and because he is so poor that he cannot get a doctor promptly, the child dies. Unconsciously, but with the certainty of cause and effect, that wasteful and luxurious woman has helped to kill the child."

THE NEW CHRISTIANITY

In the same way Professor Rauschenbusch would show that the crowded and unsanitary tenement is a sin for which the whole city suffers the punishment of tuberculosis and other diseases. The punishment of the ruined woman infects the homes of the rich equally with those of the poor. The punishment of debauched politics finally but inevitably leads to the ruin of the fairest city and the finest civilization. No man can sin by himself nor be saved by himself.

"It is not Christian to pay the lowest wages to the man who has the hungriest family."

CONVICTING SOCIETY OF ITS SINS.

All the present teaching, whether within the churches or outside of them, of the responsibility of society for the ruin of child workers, for low-paid women, for the criminal, for the wasteful rich man, for sickness and want and shame and ugliness, are all in the way of convicting humanity of its social sins. The present moral wave, which is beginning to sweep this country, is an evidence of such a conviction of sin.

The next step in religious life, after conviction of sin, is "salvation," a turning about, a new life. Just as, in the old evangelism, the individual has to be "born again," so the new evangelism demands a new birth for society. A complete change must take place; a new spirit must fire humanity. And every man and every organization, whether church-leader, or socialist, or labor agitator, or publicist, or business man, who has a vision of the new time and is working toward it, is a new evangelist.

But what will this regenerate society be like? What is, then, the vision of the prophets? I give here the conviction of Professor Rauschenbusch.

THE REBIRTH OF SOCIETY.

In the old society—the society we know now—the great sins are war, strife, competition—with resulting luxury for a few and want for many. The new social life, then, should change all this, should be a right-about-face—if it is to be true rebirth. There must be peace, not war; coöperation, not competition; and in place of extremes of luxury and want, a distribution of property which will assure every human being upon this earth a chance to make the most of the faculties God has given him.

This is the new preaching of repentance and this the new vision of salvation. And every hour it is enthralling new souls with the possibilities of love and service.

In fact, it is to bring about in society at large the spirit of the family, at its best and finest, as we now know it—the coöperation of strong and weak, old and young, the service of all by each and each by all. It seeks to make humanity one great family.

"The father," says Professor Rauschenbusch, "does not seize the larger part of the turkey and call it profit."

Nor are wages paid in the family; the turkey is not monopolized by the strong, nor are the little ones and the weak ones compelled to go hungry.

In the last chapter of his book Professor Rauschenbusch boldly meets many of the specific problems of the day. He believes with the Socialists that the wages system must ultimately be superseded by coöperation.

"I am frank to declare my conviction," he

says, "that the wages system is an institutionalized denial of the essential principles of Christianity, and that a nation will never be a Christian nation until its economic life is organized on a coöperative basis."

Professor Rauschenbusch looks forward to seeing a coöperative ownership of public utilities and ultimately the control by society of the chief means of production.

THE PART OF RELIGION IN THE NEW LIFE.

Such is the new evangelism. What part must the church and religious leaders play in it? A very great part, Professor Rauschenbusch believes. The present decadence of church influence and leadership he attributes to lack of the new vision, so that much of the prophecy, many of the noblest works in the new evangelism, have been left to men and women who are outside of the churches. The trouble has been that the church has been too anxious to magnify itself, too little concerned in humanity.

"The mischief begins when the church makes herself the end. She does not exist for her own sake; she is simply a working organi-

THE NEW CHRISTIANITY

zation to create the Christian life in individuals and the kingdom of God in human society."

Religion, in short, must become "less an institution and more a diffused force." More and more the state, society at large, will be shot through and through with the spirit of religion, and yet there will never be a time, says Professor Rauschenbusch, when there will not be a wide field of activity for the religious leader and teacher.

Two great functions will still occupy his attention. He will always fill the office of prophecy; he should be sensitized morally, so that he will be the first to discern wrong and evil, and his visions will fire the souls of men. And he will also follow behind the rumbling wheels of the chariot of state and gather up the wounded, and comfort the broken-hearted. Jesus perfectly combined both of these offices.

A NEW AMERICAN CHURCH.

As to the churches in America, Professor Rauschenbusch sees two great tendencies or drifts of development. He thinks that a great national church of America is already

THE SPIRITUAL UNREST

A PRAYER FOR BUSINESS MEN

BY WALTER RAUSCHENBUSCH

We plead with thee, O God, for our brothers who are pressed by the cares and beset by the temptations of business life. We acknowledge before thee our common guilt for the hardness and deceitfulness of our commercial life, which leads so many into temptation and causes even the righteous to slip and fall. So long as it must be that man is set against man in a struggle for wealth, help them to make their contest in some measure a test of excellence, by which even the defeated may be spurred to better work. If any man is pitted against those who have forgotten fairness and honesty, help him to put his trust resolutely in the profitableness of sincerity and uprightness, and, if need be, to accept loss rather than follow the others on crooked paths. Establish in unshaken fidelity all who hold in trust the wealth of others. The property and welfare of our nation are controlled by our business men. Help them to realize that they have high public functions and let them not betray the interests of all for their own enrichment. Grant them far-sighted patriotism to subordinate their work to the public weal, and a steadfast determination to transform the disorder of the present into the nobler and freer harmony of the future. Let the spirit of Christ, which goes out from thee and which is ceaselessly pleading within us, prevail to bring our business life under Christ's law of service, that all who guide the processes of factory and trade may feel that high consciousness of a divine calling which blesses only those who are the free servants of God and the people, and who are consciously devoting their strength to the common good.

THE NEW CHRISTIANITY

A PRAYER FOR CHILDREN WHO WORK

BY WALTER RAUSCHENBUSCH

O thou great Father of the weak, lay thy hand tenderly on all the little children on earth and bless them. Bless our own children who are the life of our life, and who have become the heart of our heart. Bless every little child-friend who has leaned against our knee and refreshed our soul by its smiling trustfulness. Be good to all children who crave in vain for human love, or for flowers and water, and the sweet breast of Nature. But bless with a threefold blessing the young lives whose slender shoulders are already bowed beneath the yoke of toil, and whose glad growth is being stunted forever. Let not their little bodies be utterly sapped, and their minds given over to stupidity and the vices of an empty soul. We have all jointly deserved the mill-stone of thy wrath for making these little ones to stumble and fall. Grant all employers of labor stout hearts to refuse enrichment at such a price. Grant to all the citizens and officers of States which now permit this wrong the grace of holy anger. Help us to realize that every child in our nation is in very truth our child, a member of our great family. By the holy Child that nestled in Mary's bosom, by the memories of our own childhood joys and sorrows, by the sacred possibilities that slumber in every child, we beseech thee to save us from killing the sweetness of young life by the greed of gain.

developing. He sees the great Protestant bodies—Presbyterians, Baptists, Methodists, Congregationalists and others—drawing rapidly together. Without essential differences of belief, with constant exchange of ministers, with a spirit of fraternity in public work, Professor Rauschenbusch sees them all drawing together, becoming less insistent upon the church as an organization but seeking rather to make it far more pervasive as an influence. The American church will be the great religious body animating the American democracy.

On the other hand, he sees a smaller group, including Roman Catholics, part of the Lutheran and part of the Episcopal bodies, drawing together on a more closely-knit basis of church organization, based upon external authority.

We talked somewhat of the methods of the new evangelism. It was Professor Rauschenbusch's conviction that one of the chief requirements would be the constant and luminous setting forth of the facts regarding present-day conditions; but he also thinks that important changes will be necessary in re-

THE NEW CHRISTIANITY

ligious expression and worship. As the old evangelism developed its songs, its prayers, its forms of exhortation and worship, so will the new. And they will not be less but more profoundly religious than the old. Professor Rauschenbusch is himself writing a small book of prayers which he hopes may help those interested in the new evangelism. Two of these prayers are reproduced with this chapter. Nothing could better reveal the quality of Professor Rauschenbusch's spirit nor present his message more convincingly.

THE END

INDEX

INDEX

Addams, Miss Jane, 236
Adler, Dr. Felix, 111, 135, 233
Alcoholism, Its Treatment, 211
Almsgiving, 251
American Magazine, Preface
American Rabbis, 138
Ark of the Covenant, 4
Asher, Rabbi, 136
Atonement, Jewish Day of, 119, 120
"Awful" Gardner, 144

Baptists, 284
Baptist Theological Seminary of Rochester, 265
Barbour, William D., 165
Barker, Dr. of Johns Hopkins, 204
Barkley, Rev. Dr. J. M., 59
Bates, Rev. H. Roswell, 35, 157
Batten, Dr., 87, 89
Bellamy, 267
Beloit College, 93
Boston, Jews in, 109
Brick Church, 167, 168
Broadway, Trinity Church, 6
Broadway Tabernacle, 52
Buildings, Fine Church, 99

Cabot, Dr. Richard C., 204, 223, 225
Cahan, Abraham, 139
Carnegie, Andrew, 63
Cathedral, Middle Age, 79, 113, 250
    St. John the divine, 78, 79

INDEX

Census, Church, 59, 60
Chapin, Prof. Robert Coit, 93
Charities Directory, 15
Charity Organization Society, 254
Chedarim, 121
Chicago, 109, 234, 251
Choate, Joseph H., 40
Christ Church, 164, 165, 166, 171, 173
Christian Endeavor Society, 67
Christianity, 108, 127, 273
" Christianity and the Social Crisis," 263, 266, 268
Christian Science, 64, 194
Church, 25, 47, 57
    of the Ascension, 87, 90
    Business Methods of, 64, 65
    Contributions to, 64, 65, 66, 67
    Definition of, 4
    Discontent among church workers, 51
    of England Protestant, 6
    Influences — causes of Decline, 69
    of Most Precious Blood, 34
    of New York, 50, 56
    In Rural Districts, 58
    of the Sea and Land, 157
Churchman, The, 42, 60
Clark University, 230
Cochran, Rev. Dr., 97
Cocks, Rev. O. G., 157
Conclusions, 230
Confession, 222
Convicting Society of Its Sins, 277
Coriat, Dr. Isador H., 204

Davies, Dr. Henry, 60
Davis, Philip, 117

INDEX

Dawson, Rev. W. J., 90
Decline of Country Churches, 56, 57
De Forest, R. W., 22
Dependent Missions, 72
De Witt Memorial Church, 157
Disease, 200, 256
Disease of Unearned Property, 14
Dix, Rev. Dr., 39
Dowie, Rev. Alexander, 191, 193, 194, 202
Dowkontt, Rev., 157
Duane Methodist Church, 84

Easter Sunday, 180
Eddy, Mrs. Mary Baker G., 192, 194, 202
Effort Toward New Forms of Religious Expression, 125
Elliott, Dr. John Lovejoy, 233, 237, 238, 243, 244, 250
Elsing, Rev. W. T., 159
Emigrants, 235
Emmanuel Baptist Church, 84
Emmanuel Church, 184, 203, 207, 219
Emmanuel Movement, 89
    Basis, 198, 205
    Beginning of, 197
    Criticisms of, 221, 227
    Cures, 204, 210, 211, 213, 214, 215, 226
    Description of, 183, 184
    Fundamental Beliefs of, 202
    Health Services, 218
    Memorial House, 185
    Methods, 207, 208, 219, 222
    Originators, 195
    Problem of, 187
    Reasons for, 221, 222
Endowments, Religious, 79, 83
Episcopal Church, 1, 11, 27, 28, 91

INDEX

Epworth League, 67
Ethical Culture Movement, 135, 139, 233
Examination as Tendency, 126

Failure of Mission Chapels, 72
Falconio, Archbishop, 54
Farr, James M., Dr., 168, 170
"Federation of Churches," 92
Fisk, Dr. A. S., 58
Flight of Protestant Churches, 69, 71, 75
Francis of Assisi, 98, 99

George, Henry, 266
Ghetto, 120
Gilder, Richard Watson, 22, 41
Government Census of Churches, 59, 60
Grace Church, 7
Greer, Bishop, 42
Grossman, Rev. Dr., 131

Hadley, S. H., 153
Hall, Prof. G. Stanley, 201, 230
Hardie, Kier, 93
Harris, Rabbi, 125
Health Services in the Church, 218
Hebrew Church, 101, 257
Hillquit, Morris, 139
Hirsch, Dr. Emil G., 132, 134
Hohoff, Mrs., 244
How the Church has Lost Its Hold, 187
Hudson Guild, 233, 236, 239, 240, 241, 242, 245, 246, 247, 248, 249, 251
Hughes, Governor Charles E., 12
Hull House, 251
Huntington, Rev. Dr., 42

INDEX

Institutional Activities, 132, 133, 169 to 173
Intellectual Evolution of a Liberal Scholar, 266
Irvine, Alexander F., 87

"Jack the Rat," 143
James, Professor William, 189, 201, 204, 205, 206
Janet, Dr. Pierre, 201
Jay, William, 10, 11
Jefferson, Rev. Chas. E., 52
Jesup, Morris K., 63
Jesus, 133, 134, 273, 281
Jews,
    Activities of, 102, 103, 104
    Alienation from Synagogues, 75, 118
    Americanizing of, 117, 120, 121
    Dietary Laws, 124, 130
    Efforts to Proselyte, 107
    Ideals and American Life, 106
    Liberalism among, 139
    Loss of Religious Strength, 55, 75
    Membership in Christian Churches, 107
    Orthodoxy, 112
    Population, 54, 102, 107
    Theological Seminary, 137
    Tribal Instincts, 113
    Unrest among, 109
Jones, Rev. Jenkin Lloyd, 127, 236
Judson, Rev. Dr., 87, 167
Jerry McAuley Mission, 142 to 162

Kennedy, John Stewart, 64
Kit Burn's "Rat-Pit," 143

Laidlaw, Dr. Walter, 52, 53, 74
Lasalle, 111
Legislature of State of New York, 1, 8

INDEX

"Looking Backward," 267
Lorimer, Rev. George C., 52
Lourdes, 198
Low, Seth, 40

Mack, Judge Julian W., 140
Manning, Rev. Dr., 31
Mariners' Temple, 157
Marx, Karl, 111
McAlpin Literary Society, 170
McAuley, Jerry, 144 to 154
McClellan, Mayor, 40
McComb, Rev. Dr. Samuel, 183, 186, 197, 202, 208, 214, 215, 219, 224
McMillan, Rev. F. N., 57
Mental Healing, 209
Methodist Church Extension Society, 80
Methodists, 252
Meyer, Rev. Louis, 107
Middle Age Cathedrals, 79, 113, 250
Mills, D. O., 63
Ministers, 53, 84, 186, 188
Missions, 67, 71, 72, 80, 108, 127, 168
Mitchell, Dr. Weir, 204, 230
Moss, Frank, 257
Municipal Art Commission, 40
"My Religion," 267

New American Church, 281
New Evangelism, 275
New Idealism, 190, 191
New York Art Commission, 40
New York Central Railroad, 246
New York City, 20, 49, 51, 69, 98, 101, 102, 104, 113, 117, 175, 176, 181, 234, 256, 257

INDEX

New York City Mission, 70, 71
New York Colony, 6
Number of Churches, 82
Nurses' Settlement, 234

Observer, The, 58
Olivet Memorial Church, 71
Osler, Dr., 201
Overwork and Underfeeding, 93

Parkhurst, Rev. Dr., 257
Parsons, Herbert, 165
Parsons, John, 39, 195
Paulist Fathers, 82
Pauperism, 255
Peckham, Judge, 21
Peters, Rev. Dr., 257
Phipps Fund, 229
Population, 53, 102
Poverty, 255
Powell, Rev. Lyman P., 209 to 213, 217
Prayer for Business Men, 282
Prayer for Children Who Work, 283
Presbyterians, 284
Presbyterian Synod of Ohio, 57
"Progress and Poverty," 266
Protestants, 74, 75
Protestant Churches, 51, 73
    Alienation from, 56, 60
    Buildings, 54
    Lack of Convictions, 92
    Membership, 53
    Methods of, 76, 77
    New Activities, 87, 88
    No Message for Common People, 96

INDEX

    Poor Attendance, 81, 82
    Statistics, 65, 80
    Uptown Movement, 55
Putnam, Dr. James J., 227

Queens Farm, 7, 9
Quinby, P. P., 192

Rainsford, Rev. Dr., 52, 87, 167
Rauschenbusch, Prof. Walter, 260, 263, 264, 269 to 284
Reaction Toward Orthodoxy, 137
Rebirth of Society, 278
Reform Jews, 129–135
Reform Movement, 129, 130, 131, 132
Relieving Pain, 213
Religion, 5, 31
    and Disease, 224, 225
    and New Life, 280
Religious Element, The, Preface
Revivals, 90, 162, 262
Rich and Poor, 94, 95
Rockefeller, J. D., 62
Roman Catholic Church, 34, 54, 63, 188, 252, 284
Roosevelt, Theodore, 40
Root, Elihu, 40
Rosenthal, Lessing, 140
Rosenwald, Julius, 141

Sabatier, Paul, 79, 250
Sage, Mrs. Russell, 63
Salvation Army, 67
Schechter, Dr. Solomon, 137
Schiff, Jacob H., 137, 141
Settlements, 89, 181
Silverman, Rev. Dr., 131
Sing Sing, 144